Praise for *The Story of Purpose*

"*The Story of Purpose: The Path to Creating a Brighter Brand, a Greater Company and a Lasting Legacy*, is thought provoking, stimulating and a must-read for any business leader."

—**Carol Tomé**
CFO, The Home Depot

"There is no one more passionate about purpose than Joey Reiman. I am grateful I let some of that passion wear off on me in the years I led Newell Rubbermaid. If you are not sure where purpose belongs on your leadership priority list, you need to read this (*The Story of Purpose*). I entered the working world in an era when the application of business psychology was just coming into vogue. While still sound, this is no longer enough. As a leader, you can continue to own and manage the motivation of your organization, or you can choose to unleash an inspiration and conviction that will be self-motivating— your organization's authentic purpose. The choice seems obvious. If you are ready to get started, read *The Story of Purpose*."

—**Mark D. Ketchum**
Former CEO, Newell Rubbermaid

"Purpose drives profit. Meaning makes money. Companies have souls. The challenge is to find that soul, define that purpose, and begin leading your organization with this as the core of everything. Joey's gift is to help leaders through this journey to unlock their company's true potential by reminding them who they really are."

—**Rilla Delorier**
EVP, Chief Marketing Officer, SunTrust Bank

"Adjunct Professor Reiman has been teaching students the power purpose at Goizueta Business School for more than a decade. If the reception of *The Story of Purpose* is anything like his class, expect a global transformation of the way we think about business and the positive role it can play in society."

—**Larry Benveniste**
Dean of Emory University's Goizueta School of Business

"True to his nature, Reiman has produced a book that is witty, colorful, wise, and fun. However, don't let that fool you to the fact that this book has a very important message for all who seek to create a model of business that fits the world's deepest hungers in this century. When has feeding the world's deepest hungers ever been a recipe for anything other than great business? Reiman knows the answer to that question, and you should read his book."

—Corey Keyes
Professor of Sociology at Emory University

"Joey Reiman has the rare gift of finding the hidden treasure in the wilderness of neglected details. Who would have thought that the master idea that would offer renewal to business would be the recovery of purpose? Joey regularly performs magic by discovering an institution's hidden virtues and values."

—Sam Keen
Philosopher, author of *Fire in the Belly*

"Joey Reiman is the big bang of thinkers. *The Story of Purpose*, a profound business book, is almost a stellar physics book in that Reiman's theory is that 'purpose is as big a force as gravity.' Enlightening!"

—Bob Berman
Astronomer, author of *The Sun Beats*

"In a world in which corporations are legal persons, Joey Reiman has made a career of encouraging businesses to know themselves and define their distinctive identities and purposes, without which they are sociopathic, and to understand their purposes in a context of interdependence. He has envisioned a maturing of the corporate world in which business can become a resource for sustainability and peace. The outcome remains uncertain, but if business is not working toward a viable and just world, we are unlikely to arrive there."

—Mary Catherine Bateson
Author of *Composing a Further Life: The Age of Active Wisdom*

"Joey Reiman's ability to unlock business truths is unrivalled. This time he asks the question: What drives business success? Reiman skillfully examines the evolution of business practices and concludes that to create profit without purpose is to create the empty noise of a false prophet. Rather profit must be the servant of *purpose* if is to truly unlock the engine that will supercharge business performance and in the process create a better humanity. *The Story of Purpose* will stand alongside *Built to Last* as a defining work for business thinkers in the twenty-first century."

—Michael Greenlees
Board Member, Abercrombie & Fitch;
CEO, Ebiquity plc, London;
CEO, TBWA Worldwide;
Executive Vice President, Omnicom Inc. (1998–2002)

"Joey Reiman continues to demonstrate his deep understanding of the essence of creating and maintaining a strong brand. Purpose. It's critical. Every company needs to have a clear purpose in order to succeed in such a competitive environment. I love that he states 'It's not just about getting ahead but having a heart.' In his book, Joey is able to clearly lay out how companies can get there."

—Brian Dyson
Former Vice Chairman and Chief Operating Officer,
The Coca-Cola Company;
Founder and President of Chatham International Corporation

"Reiman has taken the twinning of 'doing well' and 'doing good' to a new level. He demonstrates that the fundamental force in our lives, the drive to find a purpose, is also the fundamental force in successful marketing and ultimately in a successful business—but only if we can find a way to harness that force and to direct it. *The Story of Purpose* shows us that way."

—Fred Lawrence
President, Brandeis University

"*The Story of Purpose*, Joey Reiman's latest and most important book, is both compelling and confrontational. Perhaps his most compelling insights suggest that business, as a human collective, has an important choice to make: discover a sense of purpose and define a mission that makes the world a better place, or engage in trivial competition and meaningless growth that spawns success without significance. For over two decades, Joey's firm, BrightHouse, has been in the business of helping its clients make the right strategic choice to achieve true significance for all their stakeholders. The beauty of this book is that it shares the lessons of this experience and provides a grounded, practical guide to help business organizations rediscover themselves and activate a purpose-based organization that can attain significance and meaning while allowing the world to truly prosper."

—Roderick Gilkey
Emory University Professor, Joint Appointment in
Schools of Business & Medicine

"The Story of Purpose teaches us that there are two currencies in self-enlightened capitalism, money and meaning. The latter being the richer. Joey and I are in the same business. Canyon Ranch brings health and well-being to individuals. *The Story of Purpose* does the same for brands and companies. Reiman is a prophet for how to make profit in the age meaning."

—Mel Zuckerman
Founder and Chairman of Canyon Ranch

"Executives the world over now realize that brands and consumers now live in an always on, information overloaded and hyperconnected world where brands can no longer control their message or how or when a consumer can interact with a brand. Reiman delivers the perfect antidote for brands in an age of transparency, clutter and confusion."

—Alan Herrick
CEO & CO-Chairman, Sapient Corporation

"I have witnessed Joey Reiman in the college classroom and consulting in the boardroom—he always acts with creativity, caring, and clarity. In *The Story of Purpose* he is able to channel these wonderful qualities into a book that will both inspire and inform. Read this book, but more important, embrace its purpose—to provide you the model and tools to live a life of meaning."

—Jeff Rosensweig
Professor Goizueta Business School;
Former Chairman, Emory University Ethics Center

THE STORY OF

PURPOSE

THE STORY OF

PURPOSE

THE PATH TO CREATING
A BRIGHTER BRAND,
A GREATER COMPANY, AND
A LASTING LEGACY

JOEY REIMAN

WILEY

John Wiley & Sons, Inc.

Published by John Wiley & Sons, Inc., Hoboken, New Jersey.
Published simultaneously in Canada.

Library of Congress Cataloging-in-Publication Data:

Reiman, Joey.
   The story of purpose: the path to creating a brighter brand, a greater company,
and a lasting legacy/Joey Reiman.
   Includes index.
   ISBN: 978-1-118-44369-9 (cloth); ISBN: 978-1-118-46397-0 (ebk);
   ISBN: 978-1-118-46399-4 (ebk); ISBN: 978-1-118-46398-7 (ebk)
      1. Organizational effectiveness.   2. Organizational change.   3. Social
responsibility of business.   4. Branding (Marketing)   I. Title.
   HD58.9
   658.4'06–dc23

                                                              2012035105
Printed in the United States of America
10 9 8 7 6 5 4 3 2 1

To My Purpose in Life:
Cynthia, Alden and Julien

Contents

About the Cover

The Venn diagram that appears on this book's cover was invented by John Venn as a way of picturing relationships between different groups of things. For purposes of illustrating purpose, the diagram illustrates Aristotle's axiom "where your unique talents and the needs of the world intersect, therein lies your vocation." In other words, where your talents as an organization and the needs of the world intersect, therein lies your purpose.

World-class designer, Joe Paprocki, www.paprocki andco.com, who has shared his talents with me for 20 years, created this cover. I am glad we intersected.

Foreword

A foreword should have a distinctive purpose, a reason for the reader to spend his or her time and hard-earned money for a book. That's why I agreed to write this one for thought leader and purpose visionary Joey Reiman, whom I once referred to as the Moses of marketing.

As a professor of marketing at one of the most prestigious business schools in the world, the Kellogg School of Management at Northwestern University, I have seen marketing models come and go. This one is here to stay.

Beyond wealth creation and shareholder value is an unlimited resource to create a better world and a lasting legacy for businesspeople around the globe. It's called purpose.

Although the concept of purpose is not new, Joey Reiman's application and its promise for business are. No longer can pure profit be the sole reason for business creation. Capitalism needs a reset and purpose, or soulful excellence as Reiman calls it. Purpose is the catalyst that can reinvigorate and empower capitalism.

Marketing will benefit greatly as brands take stands in a world that will no longer stand for a glut of commoditized products and services without meaning.

This is not a warning for marketers but an opportunity. First there was the product benefit, then came the emotional benefit. Reiman and I, along with others, now herald in the societal benefit that organizations are capable of delivering when they believe they have a greater responsibility in the world.

These purposeful brands and companies will indeed transform society by using the power of business to mitigate the ills of the world, such as hunger, poverty, injustice, and the deterioration of the environment. No other sector in society has the means to do so. It's up to us, to you. This book shows how to do it.

Reiman provides a striking and time-tested methodology for uncovering what he calls the Master Idea of a brand or company. It is based on the compelling notion that companies don't live in the past but that the past lives in them.

Their foundational character once uncovered reveals a path to a more engaged workforce, more innovative products and services, more committed customers, dramatic increases in profits, and positive societal impact.

Great riches or the richness of life can define wealth. Reiman says you don't have to choose. The only choice you have to make is whether you take part in the most promising business story in recent times.

I now join Joey Reiman and his purpose to share *The Story of Purpose*. We hope you will make it your business to share it with every company on earth.

—**Philip Kotler**
S.C. Johnson & Son Professor of International
Marketing at the Kellogg School of Management,
Northwestern University, Evanston, Illinois;
Author of *Up and Out of Poverty*; *Corporate Social
Responsibility*; *Social Marketing*; and *Marketing 3.0*.

Preface

The Story of Purpose is the next remarkable chapter for business. In this new era, purpose and meaning make for better brands, brighter companies, and lasting legacies for everyone involved.

I've spent decades consulting to many of the leading purpose leaders and top companies around the globe. As a result of my experiences, I wrote this book for individuals who want to elevate the role of business. My goal is to align companies with higher purpose to become part of a vanguard of visionaries who will transform society through the work of business.

Throughout history, people have desired meaning as much as money. Companies are now feeling that same desire, and business is bringing it on. Beyond shareholder value are unlimited resources created by businesses working toward greater purpose. This book is the culmination of 17 years of purpose theory, modeling, and application that global giants such as Procter & Gamble, McDonald's, Carlsberg, and Newell Rubbermaid are now using with great success.

My purpose—and the mission of this book—is to inspire you with the work of the world's most famous companies and equip you with the tools and strategies you need to make your organization as successful and respected as they are. Whether you are a student of business, an associate in a firm, an entrepreneur, or a chief executive officer, you will want to take part in this story.

Our journey begins at business's new dawning and enters the offices of the world's most purposeful leaders, brands, and companies to discover best practices of purpose-inspired business.

You will learn how to excavate, articulate, and activate purpose in your organizations. And by doing so, your organization can realize financial returns more than 1,000 percent better than S&P 500 companies.

You will discover a whole new language for marketing as we move from brand to stand, point of difference to point of view, big idea to Master Idea, and the new ROI: return on inspiration.

You will find out what kind of organization you are working in—a plantation, castle in the sky, fortress, or if you are one of the fortunate, the idyllic and coveted Camelot company. If you are not, you will learn the path to get there.

Most important, you will recognize the power you and your organization have to affect society in a positive and meaningful way.

The Story of Purpose shares the directions to the most exciting time and place in business and compels you to become a lead character in the story.

Introduction

Maybe stories are just data with a soul.

—Brene Brown[1]

Can business save the world? I've pondered this question for years and find that it has always remained core to a company's purpose. Against the backdrop of international terror, teetering economies, a compromised climate, and a crisis in meaning, I witness every day how business is coming to the rescue.

As the chief executive officer (CEO) of global consultancy BrightHouse and professor at the Goizueta School of Business at Emory University, I have studied for more than 30 years what makes certain companies and brands flourish. And I have consistently found that the best companies are the ones that want to make the world more successful.

Pioneering the fields of ideation and neuroscience, I have set my sights on what I call the unified theory of purpose and how business can apply it to make great contributions to humankind and all species. As a key advisor to Procter & Gamble, McDonald's, and other corporate giants, I have witnessed a superior level of leadership driven by higher callings in the world. I have concluded that the higher the individual or company's purpose, the higher his or her profit.

Purpose is both a financial and humanitarian force. Purpose-driven organizations create more good in the world, which begets greater profit, which allows them to then create even more good. It's a virtuous, never-ending circle.

Until now, the goal of business has been business: to improve the bottom line and make shareholders rich. But

1

a movement is afoot today—one that's led by new a vanguard of business leaders who believe in a greater purpose for business: to make the world a richer and more meaningful place to live.

The Story of Purpose is the story of this revolution and the growing list of leaders, companies, and brands that believe the business of business is to expand its reach and role for the betterment of society.

Part of my inspiration for telling a story rather than presenting just observations comes from whimsical *New Yorker* cartoonist Roz Chast, whose cartoon titled "Story Template" illustrates the four elements of story: "once upon a time," "suddenly," "luckily," and "happily ever after" (Figure I.1).

Once upon time, there was a big bang, a cosmic event that illustrates the power of purpose. Intent and contribution, the two characteristics of purpose, expand our universe and make important contributions, including the galaxies, the stars, the planets, and even you and me.

Suddenly, in the twenty-first century, the world loses purpose. Terror is rampant. Warming is global. Money is scarce. And meaning—the answer to questions such as, "Why we are here?"—is elusive. By the end of the century, people lose trust in their leaders, icons, and institutions.

Luckily, the institution of business comes to the rescue and focuses on creating happier, healthier people rather than just profits. Goodness is the new currency of business. A better world is the bottom line. Happily ever after, humanity reaps the rewards. Like our ever-expanding, purpose-driven universe, business growth shows no limitation to making positive contributions to all 7 billion people and the planet they inhabit.

Whether you are an astrophysicist or a marketing director, you will find that purpose creates our world. There was intention behind each contribution throughout the ages.

FIGURE I.1 "Story Template" Cartoon

Source: Roz Chast/The New Yorker Collection/www.cartoonbank.com.

Whether it is the stars above us or the cells within us, the powerful force of purpose is at work. This is its story. As Emory University professor Corey Keyes says, "Intention without contribution is blind. Contribution without intention is impotent."[2]

Story is therefore the new narrative for business. Stories shape our lives because we are why-seeking creatures. They can also tell us about the purpose of our work. Mission is a what. Vision is a where. And purpose is our why.

When members of organizations employ greater meaning, people don't get fired; they get fired up. Brands with purpose become stands. The workforce becomes a life force. Purpose teaches us that positive cause creates positive effects. And a good story is good business.

The Story of Purpose is a compass for a new direction in business. It provides the road map that will guide you in building a purpose-inspired company or brand. Using a proven and proprietary methodology and framework that has been employed by the world's most purposeful companies, you will discover your authentic purpose. It's a journey that will excavate your company's past—the fruits are in the roots—and present a truer, more modern version of your organization for today's meaning-starved marketplace.

There has never been a more exciting time to be in business, because business is now part of every human endeavor. Imagine if we all worked on purpose. It would be like experiencing the big bang, for the second time.

The Purpose

Put Humanity Back in Business

Focus on the next quarter century and the next quarter will be just fine.
—Joey Reiman,
on his economic outlook

Aristotle called it the whatness. Nietzsche called it the why. Disney called it magic. Kennedy called it the moon. Since the dawn of human thought, purpose has guided us, inspired us, and given us reason to believe in something greater.

Until now, purpose was associated with religious belief, membership in groups, dedication to a cause, and life values. But if we accept the fact that purpose is a universal force, then we must acknowledge its positive presence everywhere. Purpose is no longer confined to private reflection; it's what liberates public life.

Part I of *The Story of Purpose* sets the scene for a new transformation of business. It's an adventure story where purpose is the hero, society is at stake, and business saves the world. Purpose is the force that has the ability to tip the scales and shift from a business model that is self-serving to one that serves others.

We will witness how companies, brands, and leaders who wield purpose win on Main Street, Wall Street, and their own street, garnering the devotion of their associates.

Commerce will move from transactions to transformations, from competing to cooperating, from holding its hand out to becoming a helping hand. In this way, the twenty-first-century organization will put humanity back in business.

1

The Purpose of Work Is to Work on Purpose

Meaning makes money.

—Joey Reiman,
contemplating *The Story of Purpose*

From the Ten Commandments to David Letterman's Top 10 list, human beings have always enjoyed making lists. Guest lists, to-do lists, best-dressed lists, and best-seller lists are just a few entries on the laundry list of lists. But only one list keeps score of the capitalism race: the Fortune 500, the annual list that ranks the top 500 US companies by revenue.

Created in 1955 by *Fortune* magazine's editors as an internal resource for writers and columnists so that they'd know which companies to focus on, the Fortune 500 has been the list to get on and stay on. This list is supposed to highlight the changes and trends that are reshaping corporate America.

And that is precisely why the list is defunct.

The Fortune 500 was created in 1955, a time of prosperity and optimism in America. Business was in business for business and was putting shareholder value first. Revenue and profit at any expense helped build companies like GM, Exxon Mobil, and Walmart—the only three companies to make the number 1 spot on the list.[1] The American dream promised that if you focused your business on the bottom line, you too could make the list.

Unfortunately, when you focus only on the bottom line, everyone races to the bottom. And apparently we are there. The Gallup-Healthways Well-Being Index, which has been polling more than 1,000 adults every day since 2008, shows that Americans feel worse about their jobs today than ever before. Gallup also reports that 71 percent of our workforce is disengaged and 25 percent of this group is what they call CAVE-dwellers,[2] an acronym for consistently against virtually everything. Add 10 percent unemployment, and we have the Greater Depression—a time where the majority of businesspeople have jobs too small for their spirits.

It's time for a new list, a new definition of *success*—and a new way to measure it. We need the Purpose 500, a catalog of companies that are doing well by doing good—because it will be these companies that bring back business for good.

Author Jim Collins was famous for his 1990s business manual and manifesto for greatness. If his book is *Good to Great*, this book could be called *Great to Goodness*, a story of companies that prosper for the goodness they bring to the world.

How Packaged Goods Led to Packaging Good

A famous quote by philosopher Aristotle tells us that where one's distinctive talents intersect the needs of the world, there lies your vocation (from the Latin word *vocare*, which means "to call"[3]). The story of William Procter and James Gamble proves the Greek was right. Born in Herefordshire,

England, in 1801, William Procter worked as an apprentice learning to dip candles. At heart an entrepreneur, he began selling dry goods and eventually opened a store in London—only to be robbed shortly after. With a huge amount of debt but a larger amount of determination, he and his wife immigrated to the United States to rebuild. However, Procter's wife became sick and died shortly after their arrival in Cincinnati.

His dream now in the distance, William took a job at a bank. He quickly recognized a unique opportunity after learning that many of Cincinnati's candles were being shipped in from Philadelphia at great expense. With this insight and his earlier candle apprenticeship experience, he decided to start a candle business to pay off his debt. Cincinnati was a great place to make candles because of the fat and oil by-products from the city's huge meatpacking industry. After starting his business, William would soon marry a Cincinnati woman named Olivia Norris.

James Gamble was born in Graan, Ireland, in 1803, and his family immigrated to America in 1819 because of the widespread depression in the British Isles following the Napoleonic Wars. They were aiming for Shawneetown, Illinois, but 16-year-old James became very ill while sailing down the same river, so they took him ashore in Cincinnati and decided to settle there.

At 18 years of age, James began an apprenticeship with a soap maker and in 1828 opened his own shop. He then married none other than Elizabeth Ann Norris, sister of Olivia.

The girls' father, Alexander Norris, encouraged Gamble to form a joint venture with Procter. Both men were competing for the same meatpacking by-products to make their soap and candles, so they founded Procter & Gamble (P&G) in 1837.

Now comes the good part.

Working tirelessly, "burning the candle at both ends" (an expression that was coined much earlier, in the 1600s), the Englishman and Irishman built a pretty sweet business, and by 1859, they had reached $1 million in sales.

During the Civil War, P&G won some Union Army contracts for candles and soap, which helped light the way for a growing business and exposed more people to the quality of P&G products. In a disparate world cloaked in darkness and disease, two men offered candles and soap. Whether this act was manufactured by money or meaning is irrelevant. The fact was, for James and William, taking care of business meant taking care of others. What's more is that in the crucible of war, they found the alchemy of good—something that could create the presence of the positive.

"Touching lives and improving life" is P&G's purpose today. The primary way P&G fulfills this purpose is through brands of superior quality and value. P&G brands are a part of people's lives. They make everyday chores such as cleaning houses and bathrooms easier and even, on some occasions, enjoyable. They make literally billions of people look and feel better every day. As you will discover, the fruits are in the roots of every great brand and Purpose 500 company.

Fortune 500 companies are where money is made. Purpose 500 companies are where money goes—because people like doing business with people who care about them.

Giving Care to the Caregiver

Graco, part of Newell Rubbermaid and headquartered in Atlanta, Georgia, is the world's largest single brand of juvenile products. Their story of purpose actually defines what purpose is: an intention that creates a contribution. As we will learn, businesses without purpose might make a big profit, but brands with purpose make a big difference.

Graco's story begins on a summer night in 1955, when Mr. C. Rex Thomas watched his wife reading a book while their baby was in a swing on the front porch. His wife, who was seated in a chair, had ingeniously tied a string to the swing that rocked the baby back and forth, calming him while she read.

Mr. Thomas instantly recognized that his wife had developed a way to find a simultaneous moment of peace for herself and enjoyment for their child—and he set out to help her even more. He described his wife's innovation to his fellow tinkerer, Nate Saint, a mechanically gifted individual who figured out how to create a product that would do for Mrs. Thomas what she was trying to do for herself.

At the same time, a church friend named Robert Cone was looking for a proprietary product to build his company upon. He hired two men who he knew as tinkerers: Thomas and Saint. The three men met and created the mechanical version of Mrs. Thomas's handmade invention before the year was out. They called it the Swyngomatic.

Mothers called it a gift, since it gave them the time to read a book, eat a meal, or take a bath—that is, it gave them the opportunity indeed to take care of themselves so that they could take better care of their babies. The creation of the Swyngomatic gave birth to a new era of parenting, as it was the first product to give moms and dads some time back for themselves.

Graco was born on this simple idea—"cradle those who cradle them"—an idea that came from their origins, was conceived with intention, and made a contribution to the world. In addition, their purpose changed their customer base from babies to parents, a significantly larger market size, and refocused their acquisition strategy to parenting companies. Business increased almost 50 percent in 18 months. Today, the Graco brand is still rocking.

Purpose Brings Joy to the World

The arch is an ancient symbol for a grand human achievement, a tall order for any organization, even for McDonald's Golden Arches. Add to that the challenge McDonald's, the world's most advertised brand, faced in 2008, when it was spending marketing dollars and losing share in the United States. Customers not only had other choices, but fast food was fast becoming a no-go for parents seeking better nutrition for their families.

McDonald's needed a new course of action. So they called BrightHouse.

I was granted an audience with McDonald's cofounder Fred Turner, who agreed to meet me in Las Vegas for 1 hour. Accompanied by Neil Golden, chief marketing officer of McDonald's in the United Sates, Turner (now in his 80s) greeted me with a 1954 playbill highlighting the jazz ensemble in which he played with McDonald's cofounder Ray Kroc and the woman Kroc would eventually marry. He said, "Joey, this might help you with your work. We began our careers together as jazz players."

Turner's offering is music to my ears, since I know that the place where one begins always holds the seeds for future growth.

Indeed, the early days of McDonald's had the exuberance of a jazz session. The company was the beat, the crew was the rhythm, and the counter was the stage for the surprise. "All of us were players that interacted with the audience," Turner recalls.

Turner's insight on jazz would ultimately lead to the realization that McDonald's had lost its mojo—that surprise factor often found in jazz where one member steps out to surprise the audience. To strike a new chord with its customers, our challenge was to bring back the joy that made McDonald's what it was: the surprise of great food, a smile, and a joyful meal. Like jazz musicians inspired by the crowd and beat of the music, McDonald's started to jam with their customers again.

At the birth of every organization is an instructive spark of fire like the one we found at McDonald's. Ignited by its founders, this flame lights the way forward. This starting point is a key building block for discovering your organization's guiding purpose. If you can tune into this, the rest will naturally follow.

We learned over the next 16 weeks that McDonald's early days were all about delivering surprise to families with the promise of consistency. And like the sound of a jazz band, the theme of family and playing together became the primary goal. McDonald's is, in fact, a family, with members worldwide in 119 countries.

There's the family in the restaurant, and then there's the family behind the counter. Their job from this day forth would be to develop a truer, more modern version of their job on day 1 in 1955—to fill families with joy.

This is what would lead the organization to a joyful meal, one that would shift their focus from toys to joys. You see, the Happy Meal made McDonald's the largest distributor of toys. Then, in one of the boldest moves since the creation of the Happy Meal, McDonald's began to offer Fruit & Maple Oatmeal and the Fruit & Walnuts salads, making it the largest restaurant apple purchaser in the United States. By adding fruit to every Happy Meal, McDonald's turned purpose into practice.

By filling families with joy, McDonald's in the United States successfully moved from a brand that people just bought to a stand that people buy into. Joy has more dividends in profits and people. McDonald's stock had a meteoric increase and *Fortune* magazine put now-former chief executive officer (CEO) Jim Skinner on their executive "dream team."

As their catchy tagline says, "i'm lovin' it."

■ ■ ■

From Brand to Stand

Herders invented branding. By branding their cattle, cowboys would know what they owned. Until recently, marketing had not come much further. We were still telling consumers about the brands we owned and sold.

Media were consuming consumers. About 7,500 messages bombarded us daily with promises of health, wealth, and fame. These attacks come from what we call brands. A brand is the embodiment of all the information connected to the product serving to create associations and expectations around it. But brands are not real.

Until recently, brands were created by advertising agencies for homo consumens—those who want more and use more. But the people—organizations and those they serve—are now asking a question other than, "How much is it?" They are asking, "Why should I buy from you?" People have taken a stand. Hence, brands have followed with something extra—an authentic purpose.

Add purpose to a brand and it becomes a stand (see Figure 1.1). We no longer buy it, but rather we buy into it, because it stands for something greater. Its bar code carries a moral code, a point of view that shares a greater purpose. Stands are created from the place of origin, not from researching the marketplace for what might sell. Stands are distinctive, creating indispensability in a competitive world. As we all want to work in the company of something greater, employees take on the role of missionaries for what they stand for. Covenants, not contracts, promise people, not consumers, more ease, more care, and more love. Actions replace ads eliciting relationships between giver and receiver versus seller and buyer. The best brands, those with purpose, no longer buy media, as they have created digital communities.

A BRAND

| WHAT |
| POINT OF DIFFERENCE |
| MARKET-DRIVEN |
| COMPETITIVE |
| EMPLOYEES |
| CONSUMERS |
| CONTRACT WITH CUSTOMER |
| COMMUNICATIONS |
| ADS |
| SOCIAL RESPONSIBILITY |
| LOYALTY |
| TRANSACTIONAL LEADERSHIP |
| NEXT QUARTER |

A STAND

| WHY |
| POINT OF VIEW |
| ETHOS-DRIVEN |
| DISTINCTIVE |
| MISSIONARIES |
| ADVOCATES |
| COVENANT WITH CUSTOMER |
| COMMUNITIES |
| ACTIONS |
| SOCIAL OPPORTUNITY |
| LOVE |
| TRANSFORMATIONAL LEADERSHIP |
| NEXT QUARTER CENTURY |

PURPOSE

FIGURE 1.1 Brand versus Stand

Source: © BrightHouse. Illustration by David Paprocki.

Most exciting of all, purpose-inspired leaders are measured by their ability to transform their associates, their companies, and the world into a culture creating a place of positive presence.

These Purpose 500 companies make the world a better place. Their focus is not only sharing profit but also sharing the responsibility for a society that works better. This means acknowledging that everyone on Earth is an essential part of our collective purpose. In Martin Scorsese's Academy Award–winning picture *Hugo*, the main character shares the following perspective with his friend Isabel in the clock tower of a 1930s Parisian train station: "I like to imagine that the world is one big machine. You know, machines never have any extra parts. They have the exact number and type of parts they need. So I figure if the entire world is a big machine, I have to be here for some reason. And that means you have to be here for some reason, too."[4] Such are the human beings who make up companies of purpose.

The Story of Purpose ends a chapter for Fortune 500 companies and opens a new one for purposeful organizations that want to partner with society. "The game has changed," said Rick Gilkey, Emory University professor involved in neuroscience research in the Department of Psychiatry—and a BrightHouse luminary. "People are not motivated by the bottom line. It's about the human factor—and purpose is the driver. It's what stirs our souls and inspires us to do great things over a sustained period of time." Capitalism for these organizations capitalizes on human enterprise, not performance metrics. On people, not consumers. On relationships, not transactions. And on becoming the best company for the planet, not just on the planet.

What Is the Purpose of This Chapter?

- The purpose of business is not just to create value but to add value to people's lives. When we do so, our companies will profit in the short term, the next decade, and the world will profit in the long term, over the next century.
- Good and service are the new goods and services.
- Business is now part of every human endeavor.

Purpose Pointers

- Move from a brand to a stand.
- Turn purpose into practice.
- When purpose leads, profit follows.

2

Purpose-Inspired Leadership

Leaders follow people.

—Joey Reiman,
on leadership

The purpose-driven leader puts purpose first. Becoming such a leader begins with the desire to have a *purposeful* life and career. Neither cornering the market nor obtaining a corner office motivates purpose-filled leaders. For them, life is not printed on dollar bills.

The word *motive* comes from the Latin *motivum*, which means "moving cause."[1] A meaningful motive truly serves as the engine that fuels the purpose leader's passion. An impassioned heart is the best stimulus package. As Albert Einstein wrote, "Only one who devotes himself to a cause with his whole strength and soul can be a true master. For this reason mastery demands all of a person."[2]

The old guard leaders' symbol was the yardstick that measured how much ground his employees or company lost or won. The purpose leader's symbol is the compass to keep him or her heading in the right direction. Without purpose, leaders drift. With purpose, they steer.

Purpose leaders believe that all people are created equally important and that equality is the glue of company solidarity. Yvon Chouinard, founder of purpose-powered outdoor-enthusiast company Patagonia, stated in *Let My People Go Surfing*, "The best leadership is by example. Malinda's and my office space is like everyone else's, and we always try to be available. We don't have special parking places for ourselves or for any upper management; the best spaces are reserved for fuel-efficient cars, no matter who owns them."[3] The fact is that people want to look up to their leaders; however, they don't want those leaders to look down at them.

In a story titled *The Journey to the East* by German-Swiss poet and novelist Hermann Hesse (a favorite story of Bob McDonald's, chief executive officer [CEO] of Procter & Gamble), we learn about the role of a purpose leader through a character called Leo. Leo appears to be one of the servants for the journey who, in Hesse's words, "he did his work gaily, usually sang or whistled as he went along, was never seen except when needed—in fact, an ideal servant."[4] Throughout the book, we see Leo helping the group accomplish their journey by serving them. At the end of the journey, we realize that Leo was actually the leader of the expedition.

Purpose leaders are meaning machines that make our work important instead of banal. They are dealers of hopes and dreams. And they know that they must think large if they are going to affect the world at large. There is a story that beautifully illustrates this point. Legend has it that Sony founder and CEO, Akio Morita, met with a small group of men in a burned-out Tokyo department store in the wake of World War II. Morita's advisors presented a strategy for building a fledgling Sony. The plan would make Sony the number 1 technology company in Japan. However, Morita didn't see this as the company's goal.

He changed the mission to make *Japan the number 1 technology country* in the world.[5]

Most organizations today are overmanaged and underled. Purpose leaders don't manage; they mesmerize. They don't execute initiatives; they lead crusades. Their brands are not labels but flags that should evoke the kind of patriotism we have for the countries we live in. Think about your country's flag. Then think about your company's logo. How can your logo enlist the loyalty and fervor of your national colors? These leaders want to change the way the planet works—or as Apple's Steve Jobs is widely quoted saying, "to make a dent in the universe."

We Need More Jobs

If we want to create more jobs, we need more leaders like Steve Jobs. While he was here, Jobs created a world that we had never seen before. And with that universe came new creative professions and expressions. Apple and Pixar animated entire industries, creating work for thousands and dreams for millions. Jobs gave permission to a global generation to think differently. His mixture of precision and passion created a corporate creative combustion at Apple, which formed the most valuable company on Earth. Jobs had what the Greeks considered the highest honor, kleos: remembrance in one's own time.[6]

There's been a great deal written about other purpose leaders: Southwest Airlines' Herb Kelleher, Whole Foods Market's John Mackey, Facebook's Mark Zuckerberg, GE's Jeffrey Immelt, Google's Sergey Brin, Avon's Andrea Jung, and Ben & Jerry's Ben Cohen and Jerry Greenfield. Every one of these individuals leads with plaintiff purpose; their stories are well documented in countless books and case studies.

My desire, however, is to identify an unusual suspect—a leader in a company large enough to positively impact all of society, someone with a high command of purpose but with a name you might not recognize because of his or her humility.

Procter's Gamble

I met Procter & Gamble (P&G) CEO Bob McDonald in his conference room on the eleventh floor of the world's largest consumer packaged goods company on his 32nd anniversary with the company. And the first words out of his mouth are, "Purpose is what has made this company successful for 175 years."

A former Boy Scout, West Point Cadet, and US Army Captain in the 82nd Airborne Division, McDonald joined P&G because he found the purpose and values of the company—"to touch and improve lives"—to be similar to his own.

Growing up in Gary, Indiana, McDonald recounts being "inoculated in family values, church on Sunday and uncompromising parents when it came to honor and service." He informs me, "I was measured by what I did for others." And these early lessons come across clearly in the kind of company he now runs—because this is how this leader measures his brands and people.

Shooting for the Moon and the Stars

As McDonald explains, "West Point taught me that character is the most important trait of a leader. I define character as always putting the needs of the organization above your own." He also learns to choose "the harder right instead of the easier wrong," a line straight out of the West Point Cadet Prayer.

McDonald sat in the second row of his class at West Point, a position that indicates that a person is at the top of the class. He graduated thirteenth out of 2,000, which meant he was a Star Man. Reaching the top 5 percent in one's class comes with the honor of brandishing five stars on your collar. And despite being deployed to desert, jungle, and Arctic warfare programs, McDonald managed to complete his master's in business administration (MBA) program.

Running P&G, however, might be McDonalds's biggest test of all. He and his leadership team are charged with growing this $80 billion-plus company in the most difficult economic environment of the past several decades, while simultaneously investing for P&G's future growth, especially in developing markets. It is a difficult balance that often requires McDonald and his team to do what he learned at West Point: to choose "the harder right instead of the easier wrong."

P&G Pampers the World

Pampers is a role model for purpose. Pampers was first positioned as a disposable diaper, but Pampers turns out to be an indispensable idea for society. A brand with a purpose is no longer distinguished by a point of difference but rather by a point of view. To date, Pampers has raised funds for 300 million vaccines, protecting 100 million moms and their babies in 32 countries. The "1 pack = 1 vaccine" program has helped eliminate maternal and neonatal tetanus in eight countries, including Uganda and Myanmar.

McDonald is confident. Due to the efforts of P&G and UNICEF working hand in hand, neonatal tetanus will all but disappear by 2015, a target set by UNICEF and the World Health Organization (WHO).

Starting with the overall P&G brand, individual brands add points of view to their points of difference, one by one. Approximately 40 percent of world trade is done by multinational companies like P&G. Together they have annual sales that are larger than the gross national product of more than one-third of the countries in the world. And according to McDonald, "This gives us the responsibility and opportunity to do more."

We see leaders at the brand level developing points of view as well. Male grooming product Old Spice's point of view is that the brand should help men navigate manhood. Bounty paper towels and napkins are here to take on the messes created by the bounty of life. Feminine hygiene brand Always, among other activities, works to teach young girls in Kenya about menstruation to keep them in school; Secret deodorant brand's point of difference is fearlessness of sweating, and its point of view is to help women become more fearless of life.

Detergent Tide enacts its point of view through its mobile Loads of Hope program. Tide's mobile laundromat spins across the country to clean clothes and provide comfort during times of distress. On the road for more than three years, beginning with its journey to New Orleans after Hurricane Katrina, Tide, at no extra cost, washes, dries, and folds the clothes of thousands of families in need. Something so seemingly simple, something often overlooked during disasters—clean clothes—makes an enormous difference in the lives of those affected. Tide took their gift, that of cleansing, and made it into a mission.

The bottom line according to McDonald is that "purpose attracts people." To prove it, the company commissioned research firm Millward Brown to conduct a global study of key attributes of best brands, whose findings thrilled McDonald and me. Here is a quote from the 2007 study:

> Best brands transcend consumer segments and regional markets by rooting their brand in universal values. They create and occupy a mental space that goes beyond the product or the category. They serve a bigger purpose.

"Purpose creates so much meaning. It turns jobs into callings," extols McDonald. "That's because they are truisms. When you find a truism in today's world, it's easy to discount it. But don't walk away from it."

Truth becomes a prevailing theme in our dialogue. Authenticity is critical in the world of purpose in business. You will quickly learn that if your purpose is not authentic— if it does not come from the *ethos* of the enterprise—then it will not serve the organization. All too often marketers make up a brand's purpose based on what they think the market wants. What the marketplace wants is honesty and genuineness. When you are real, people know it, feel it, and buy it.

Purpose Leaders Inspire Purpose

Amicus curiae is Latin for "friend of the court"[7]—the king's trusted advisor. I ask leaders during our conversations to imagine whom those confidants might be. I posed this question to McDonald. Who would sit in his boardroom to advise and oversee his purpose administration? McDonald answered:

"Deng Xiaoping. When you go to China and visit the Forbidden City, you see Mao. But Xiaoping brought more people out of poverty than any leader on earth." Across from him would sit Lee Kuan Yew, first prime minister of the Republic of Singapore. "He was willing to do anything to serve others." And next to me is former Secretary of State

Henry Kissinger, who McDonald says is "the ultimate win/ win guy." He recalls the epic meeting between Kissinger and Zhou Enlai in which the statesman Kissinger tells the premier, "Let's not shake the world; let's build it."[8]

Purpose Leaders Follow Their Star

McDonald's favorite play is *The Man of La Mancha*, based on the novel by Miguel De Cervantes. It's a story about an old man who puts on a suit of rusty armor, thinks he is a knight, and calls himself Don Quixote de La Mancha. He saw the world not as it was, but as it should be—a world of caring acts, noble deeds, and impossible dreams.

McDonald believes our world, the real world, should be the same. And companies have a greater role to play in making it that way. By developing products that make a positive difference in people's lives, companies can make the world a safer and better place. Whether it's a soap that safeguards children, a detergent that turns the tide on a disaster, or a deodorant that thinks mean stinks, the greater purpose of business is no longer a dream.

Banking on Purpose

Meeting Rilla Delorier you would first be struck by her 6-foot stature, athletic build, and confidence. You can tell that she is a competitor—a result of not only her college volleyball background but also her desire to win in the field of business.

I was sitting in Delorier's expansive corner office on the executive floor of the SunTrust Plaza in Atlanta, Georgia, which she had made her own by displaying works of art produced by her two young daughters.

Delorier, named one of the most powerful women to watch in banking, was banking on greater meaning for her organization. "We want to do noble work." This is a challenge, as bankers are not seen as the most caring group. But I love her vision and logic: the more care a bank deposits, the less likely you are to withdraw from being its customer.

"There is a song that I love by Bob Sima that talks about how people remember how you make them feel." She said she tries to think about that while training employees for the personal encounters they have with clients.

"Buying a home, saving for college or retirement, or dealing with illness, loss of a job, divorce, or aging parents are all times people need someone who listens, someone to trust, and someone who will encourage them to take the right steps. We want to be that someone."

Delorier believes the company's recent transformation effort has to be *multipurpose*, as her expectations are that the work bolsters SunTrust's 28,000 associates, inspires customers in more than 1,650 locations, and boosts their $250 million a year in net income (or $180 billion in assets) and share price.

She has also redefined the role of chief marketing officer. She views this role as not just a brand maker but an industry shaker. She wanted the new SunTrust platform to elevate the whole banking sector by helping bankers create transformations, not merely transactions, in people's lives.

In the beginning, SunTrust's corporate ancestor, the Trust Company of Georgia, founded in 1891, was about helping very small companies, such as The Coca-Cola Company and Disney, companies that were small at the time, with their own beginnings. And this is where her bank's ethos intersects with the soul of this banker.

Early on, Delorier wasn't able to read. This wasn't corrected until her father, along with a very special teacher, realized she was dyslexic. They spent countless hours helping her overcome her learning disability and turn it into a new ability.

Delorier leans heavily on her emotional intelligence to lead the bank to think differently. To approach problems with not just a functional focus on financial results but also on an emotional and social connection with clients and employees, which will in turn drive financial results.

As a Harvard MBA, she knows the importance of shareholder value and profitability. Yet she believes that purpose can be the fuel that motivates employees to bring a new level of commitment and compassion to their role and into each conversation with clients. "This is how service organizations can drive performance—by capturing the heads and hearts of our employees and helping them see how they can make the biggest difference for our clients."

She adds that purpose is the missing ingredient in so many business plans. "Yet it is truly the most important element to attracting employees and clients. People want to do business with companies they respect and that are making a difference. Consumers are acting with purpose; now hopefully it will get companies to build this into their strategies."

Delorier and SunTrust are about to volley their purpose across the Southeast in one of the most comprehensive purpose programs in this nation. "We are changing how we need to 'be' as an organization: changing our mission, vision, values, and guiding principles to align to their purpose. And having our employee experience reflect these new values."

She and her organization have adopted the *Be-Do-Say* framework that you'll read about later. "We are also changing what we 'do' to deliver on the purpose, by improving the client experience, aligning our volunteerism and community engagement efforts, as well as the focus of our philanthropy." As for *say*, SunTrust's advertising and new brand articulation will focus on a message of financial well-being.

"To boldly do what is right and what is needed is the most exciting transformation I have ever been a part of," says Delorier. Rilla, her first name, means babbling brook in German, a name that is befitting as this purposeful leader is cool and refreshing in a sea of bankers trying to keep their institutions afloat.

Built to Lead

William A. Burke III will not strike you as a purpose-inspired leader. He is an MBA-carrying tool guy who got his start as a retail salesman calling on independent hardware stores in the salt of the earth states Maine, New Hampshire, and Vermont. He then spent 20 years at Black & Decker before coming to Newell Rubbermaid, where he climbed the ladder to president of Newell Professional Group, responsible for more than $2 billion in annual sales.

Burke looks hard as nails. I caught up to him in Nantucket, where he had just completed a triathlon with his 17-year-old daughter Hailey. But make no mistake, purpose is in Burke's toolbox, and what he has built with it is a benevolent empire. Burke is more hero than just a leader. His people would look up to him if it were not for his insistence that they deal with him eye to eye.

I first met Burke after the purpose work I did on Graco. Burke was leading the Tools and Hardware Group of commercial brands Irwin tools and Lenox saws. I remember him commenting that it was easy to find purpose for Graco, a brand about babies, but for saws, he said, "I don't think so." Impressed with Graco's results, however, Burke agreed to take the journey—and to change the world one brand of his at a time.

The Toolbox for Purposeful Leadership

Purpose requires constant maintenance and having the right tools at your fingertips makes it easy. Below is Burke's inventory.

Hammer Home Purpose Every Day

Purpose is not a *check the box*. It is an everyday, every way commitment that communicates your charge. Too often

I run into brands that view purpose as a distraction rather than an attraction. This is due to leaders not making purpose front and center daily. Says Burke, "Lenox goes the extra mile every day because as our purpose states, *Passion cuts through*. That charge leads this organization. The thing about purposeful leadership is that it's a do-it-yourself proposition." **Is your purpose driving all communications to your stakeholders? Is it part of your dialogue with your company?**

Nail Your Values

Great leaders are led by great values. In many respects, you are the parent of a large family and it's your business to model behaviors. Your values teach your associates how to behave. Burke exemplifies values-based leadership. His father, mother, grandfather, and a Jesuit brother were instrumental in teaching him his values.

"We want to believe in something, whether it's a higher power, calling, or a greater purpose," says Burke. "When you believe, it gives you the *faith* to do things that are very difficult sometimes and to get through challenging times. You have to stay true to it and keep that faith to win long-term." **What are your values, and how are you ensuring that they get inculcated?**

Chisel Your Talent

Purposeful leadership helps others find and craft their purpose. That means your company's talents as well as those of individual associates. Burke would take disparate business units and people throughout the world and create the juggernaut called Irwin. "To watch so many groups of people who didn't have the history and legacy of Irwin come together as one had everything to do with purpose."

Almost half of Irwin sales are outside the United States, but purpose is multilingual. If it's a human truth like "All guts, all glory," it travels. That is, it makes the point that if you throw everything into your work, the glory will be yours. And it has, as Irwin results lead the industry. **What have you done to mobilize the talents of your associates and brands?**

Bolt Together the Organization

Purpose leaders focus on alignment. They are constantly tightening the linkage among ideals, values, and company objectives. In this way we are all building the same purposeful organization. "The work of purpose enabled the team and business to harness it and create guiding values." By doing that, it allowed a stronger focus, a stronger culture to be built and one that everybody could connect with. The Master Idea "Work's better behind our shield" was authentic to the distinctive shield logo of Rubbermaid Commercial Products (RCP). On paper, RCP is the leading brand of janitorial, maintenance, hospitality, and facility products such as those yellow carts that are used by workers cleaning our malls and airports. But on purpose it is a proud shield to be worn by those who are making our world more beautiful. "This is the heart of what we do and stand for," says Burke. "Purpose started as a small little spark and became a fire that lit the path forward for RCP." **How are you creating advocacy and alignment for your organization?**

Measure Purpose

Employees want to know what their leaders value and how they will be measured. Although working on purpose is a reward unto itself, being recognized for it helps build purposeful behavior. A purposeful leader is one who is true to his or her own beliefs, is transparent and authentic, and is passionate about what he or she does.

"The way I measure purpose is an engaged workforce," says Burke. Engagement scores at Lenox are ranked among the highest throughout the Newell Rubbermaid organization. And both tool brands experienced double-digit growth after purpose was implemented. **Is your employee engagement measuring up?**

Burke's Laws

- **Employ people with purpose.** Associates should embody purpose in their personal and professional lives.
- **Create advocacy and alignment.** Stakeholders need to know why they are selling their whats to their whos.
- **Engage in continuous learning.** Expand your thinking about your purpose and role in the world.
- **Use purpose as the prism.** Purpose will guide your growth and decision making.
- **Decentralize.** Purpose has an organizing energy that does not demand centralization.
- **Earn profits in a way that is consistent with the purpose.**
- **Put your faith in purpose.** When you have purpose, you have faith. When you don't, you have people who don't want to believe and things start to fall apart.

I asked Burke what's next and if he had a favorite tune. He had one answer that addressed both questions: Frank Sinatra's "Fly Me to the Moon," because it represents ambition, daring risk, and dreaming. I saw it firsthand when Burke showed his purpose films to Wall Street analysts. "They loved them," says Burke.

So I asked, "If you were not a leader of your industry, what profession would you enter?"

"I would be a priest," the Loyola University grad replied. By all measures, Burke's competition does not have a prayer.

Davids in a World of Goliaths

These stories tell us about the three characteristics of purposeful leadership: faith, family, and fearlessness. Faith gives us the capacity for greatness. Those who grow up believing in something greater are going to achieve something greater. All put family first. Loving, caring, and respect are qualities that serve not only our most intimate relationships but those in the family of humankind. And finally I was struck by a vivid presence of fearlessness as they spoke about business taking on societal challenges.

Like David in the fable of David and Goliath, these leaders are willing to take on the giant problems of the world. Instead of a slingshot, they wield their purpose-inspired organizations, and in place of a sack of stones, they carry rock-solid values.

All three also have in common something that's uncommon in a business environment, something that puts higher callings before higher earnings: they are not afraid to put purpose first. And they won't cower to pundits and cynics. Great leaders don't avoid bad. They do good.

The best financial analysts scour the street for examples of economic performance, but the next generation of businesspeople all over the world is looking for exemplars of purposeful leadership as well.

These three and the many more who join us in *The Story of Purpose* prove you can have both. These are the formidable champions of purpose and victors in the modern world of business.

Bob McDonald's Recommended Book List:
1. *Built to Last* by Jim Collins
2. *The Leader's Compass* by Ed Ruggero and Dennis Haley
3. *The Leadership Engine* by Noel Tichy
4. *Managing by Values* by Ken Blanchard and Michael O'Connor
5. *Man's Search for Meaning* by Viktor Frankl

What Is the Purpose of This Chapter?

- Leaders are the moral center of a company.
- A brand with a purpose is no longer distinguished by a point of difference but by a point of view.
- The most valuable products in the marketplace are honesty and genuineness.

Purpose Pointers

- Lead with purpose.
- Don't manage; mesmerize.
- Don't execute initiatives; lead crusades.

3

The Master Idea

Some ideas are bigger than others.

—Joey Reiman,
on ideas

My biggest idea was born out of every mother's purpose: to protect and inspire her child's spirit. I named my consultancy BrightHouse, because my mother made me a toy White House when I was eight years old. She said, "One day, Joey, you will work in the real one—maybe as president."

I didn't make it as chief executive officer (CEO) of the free world, but I *did* become the leader of an organization whose chief focus is helping business generate commercial success through social value. I managed to break through the archaic world of traditional advertising to create the world's first *ideation* firm—and I began *thinking* for a living.

Some Ideas Are Bigger Than Others

Shortly after creating BrightHouse, I received as a gift a book by Cal State East Bay professor Theodore Roszak. Upon reading Roszak's commentary on ideas, I was wildly inspired with one of my own.

Roszak calls certain ideas "Master Ideas—the great, moral, religious and metaphysical teachings which are the foundations of culture."[1] He believes that we occupy our minds with so much data that it obscures our thinking. But beneath our daily thinking lies foundational ideas that shape us. Master Ideas are not based on facts but the conviction that the thought will stir the soul.

These ideas come to us in the form of powerful statements such as "God is love," "All men (and women) are created equal," and "We shall overcome." These megawatt concepts can't be proved, but they challenge our world to work better and illuminate our lives and times. A Master Idea is a purpose with meaning. It is a signpost that originates in an organization's ethos and that points to higher ground by inspiring, guiding, and protecting. Most important, a Master Idea imbues human beings with meaning.

Master Ideas can do exactly the same for organizations. They have the animating and vital power to lift companies and their staffs, and via the work that they do, they eventually lift the world.

Enterprises that employ individuals who embrace purpose create more engagement, more money, and more ideas. Organizations built on Master Ideas are filled with people who act more like volunteers for a cause than employees going through the motions to get a paycheck. Their leaders don't just ask, "What keeps me up at night?" They also ask, "What gets me up in the morning?" The companies and brands that are powered by the profound shaping presence of a Master Idea are the ones that are reshaping the way business works and society lives.

Like the Master Ideas that have expanded our thinking and our embracing of the world at large, Master Ideas expand businesses' orbit of caring to all stakeholders. Companies in this new era have only one client: society.

In addition, Roszak cites two crucial defining characteristics of a Master Idea: it must be *infectious* and *enduring*. "Master Ideas don't come and go," he says. "They come and *stay*. The marvelous thing about Master Ideas is often when people hear them, they take them into their lives immediately."[2]

Profits are the way in which a company stays in business; they come as a result of effective execution. The Master Idea is the driving force *behind* execution. It distills all of what is great about an organization and instills in each associate that same greatness. When purpose and business unite, companies see a new ROI: return on *inspiration*. The world's most inspiring company is also the most valuable. Case in point: in 2012, Apple's capitalization is valued at $465 billion.[3]

Principles of a Master Idea

After working to bring purpose to the world's most famous companies and brands, I have identified nine key principles of Master Ideas in the corporate world. These are the criteria we use to build a Master Idea. Following are examples of each principle. A Master Idea combines all nine.

1. **The Master Idea is *timeless*.** Master Ideas are truths. Whereas facts, as well as your brand's positioning, may change over time, truth never does. Master Ideas cut across generations, fusing an organization's past with its goals and hopes for the future. Regardless of its meteoric growth, Google's Master Idea of "Don't be evil" provides both a directive and guardrails for the company.[4]

2. **The Master Idea** *teaches*. The world's best ideas make us better. They expand our thinking by providing lessons. Starbucks founder and CEO Howard Schultz taught the world a whole new language for coffee and redefined the role of the server. The barista became the "star," and the "bucks" poured in. At the time of this publication, the company boasts more than 87,000 different drink combinations; bean growers and bean counters alike have enjoyed this caffeine rush.[5]

3. **The Master Idea** *fulfills*. The Master Idea fulfills a fundamental desire in all of us. From top floor management to factory floor accomplishment, Master Ideas ignite our passions and create a sense of being *alive*. TOMS's chief shoe giver, Blake Mycoskie, touches our souls. For every purchase of TOMS, a pair of shoes goes to someone in need. TOMS, now one of the world's fastest-growing shoe companies, gets its name from its purpose: "Shoes for a better tomorrow."[6]

4. **The Master Idea is a** *battle cry*. Master Ideas are marching orders. In 1914, IBM's Founder, Thomas Watson Sr., attaches the mantra "THINK" to his brand. Almost a century later, Apple leader Steve Jobs, yells back, "Think *different*."[7] Master Ideas rally us to follow our collective ambition. Although it was never intended to be an advertising tagline, Nike's Master Idea, "Just Do It,"[8] appeals not only to those who want to win a race but to the entire human race.

5. **The Master Idea is** *based on ethos*. Like the oak tree that sprouts from an acorn, great companies grow from seeds planted in the company's beginnings. The ethos is the name of the company. Richard Branson created every Virgin enterprise with the ethos of "brand new." Virgin Produced, a film development company; Virgin Unite, the Virgin Group's charitable organization; and

Virgin Galactic, which takes wing in outer space, all create a "Virgin experience."[9] Maybe Virgin Government will be next.

6. **The Master Idea is** *transformative*. In the same way that chemical reactions transform all elements involved, Master Ideas create holistic change for an organization. Strategy moves brands from the rational to the emotional, creating a purpose that affects an entire organization. Inspired by its genius founder and inventor Thomas Alva Edison, General Electric (GE), with support from CEO Jeffrey Immelt and vice president of Aviation Systems, Lorraine Bolsinger[10], has launched a reinvented "eco-imagination" green initiative that refocuses the entire organization from best company on Earth to best company *for* Earth.

7. **The Master Idea** *inspires.* The word *spirit*—a synonym for *soul*—comes from the Latin *spiritus*, originally meaning "breath."[11] Master Ideas breathe life into people and their organizations, allowing brands and companies to become animated by greater meaning. People go to supermarkets for the fish sole; however, they go to organic grocery chain Whole Foods Market for *soul*. CEO John Mackey and his girlfriend borrowed $45,000 to open a natural foods store called Safer Way in 1978. Unable to store food in his apartment, he moved into the store. Two years later, partnering with Craig Weller and Mark Skiles, he opened Whole Foods Market, a company whose revenues exceed $10 billion today.[12] Even the story is inspiring.

8. **The Master Idea is born not from data but from** *absolute conviction*. Master Ideas are created not by research but by a search for deeper meaning. Visionary Walt Disney petitioned hundreds of banks for a loan for which many thought was a Mickey Mouse idea.

This year, through an extensive portfolio of mediums and international e-commerce, that idea will create billions of dollars in revenue.[13] Faith beats information. As the new mantra at multinational consumer goods company Unilever puts it, "More magic, less logic."[14]

9. **The Master Idea *tells a story*.** William Booth did not have time to send a holiday greeting to his offices throughout the world. As the leader of a very frugal organization, Booth searched for the shortest message he could send by telegraph. He used a one-word battle cry to inspire his associates with a lesson that has been telling people who join him why they are here for more than 100 years. That lesson launched an army—The Salvation Army. The word? "Others."[15]

A New Narrative for Business

Master Ideas are creating a new narrative for business. It is both the story of old and new—of operational excellence that measures performance metrics and of soulful excellence that measures human metrics.

Together, they are a new story for business.

Company leaders know that the power of a story can engage and inform people both inside and outside their organizations. As the story goes, when Steve Jobs and his direct reports were trying to decide whether to get into the music business, his lieutenants all told him that no, they should not. After all, that wasn't their core business. Jobs had only two questions in response to their protests: (1) "Will music someday be digital?" and (2) "Are computers digital?" Then he answered them by introducing the iPod.

If you've ever gathered with others around a campfire, you know that the fire truly brought you together and compelled people to share stories. Although you were probably surrounded by wilderness, you felt safe. Master Ideas work the same way. They create a central fire for an organization. People gather around it and share stories. Sparks fly, and the cold corporation is warmed.

Profit and loss (P&L) statements may tell of financial profits and losses. However, they don't tell the story of what people gain from recounting how they—as a team, a global business unit, or a company—built, created, stopped, helped, loved, and even lost. Investing in meaning might turn out to be a company's biggest windfall. Meaning at work *works*.

Our search for meaning has been going on since the first human opened her eyes. It's what we all have in common. So if our quest for meaning is a foundational force, why would we check it at the office door?

If we could bring our meaning to work—let alone find it there—companies would encounter missionaries in the elevators, breakthroughs in the break rooms, and thinking outside our cubicles. The C-suite gets a little sweeter, too, as companies jettison their steely-eyed, know-it-all leaders. Instead, leadership comes from a genuine human being in the moral and ethical sense—a mentor, not a tormentor.

A business with a Master Idea in its quiver is equipped for a harsh world. It wins by aiming its story to those in need. Pampers vaccinates children. Safeguard soap saves them. Lego builds them. Chrysler has taken upon itself to rebuild its home Detroit. Tide cleaned up after Hurricane Katrina. And Paper Mate is trying to make the world right by putting a pen in everyone's hand.

Business's new narrative begins with purpose, tells the story of profits, and ends with people. Money becomes a means to an end, rather than an end in itself.

"At a certain juncture in history, this idea arose in the minds of a few morally impassioned thinkers as a defiantly compassionate response to conditions of gross injustice that could no longer be accepted as tolerable," writes Roszak.[16] What if business could harness the power of these Master Ideas? If so, they could master their own destinies, muster up the untapped energy of their peoples, power up profits, and correct the ills of the society.

For centuries, religions and governments have tried to provide legends and laws to the world with hopes of improving society. Now it's business's turn. "Taking care of business" now means taking care of the world. The stories of purpose in this book illustrate just what that might look like.

What Is the Purpose of This Chapter?

- Master Ideas are the biggest ideas of all.
- Master Ideas are timeless truths that don't come and go but come and stay.
- The power of story engages and informs people both inside and outside their organizations.

Purpose Pointers

- Discover, articulate, and activate your Master Idea.
- Create a narrative for your brand.
- Share your story with the world.

The Black Box of Strategy

In every acorn, an oak; in every beginning, a purpose.

—Joey Reiman,
on where purpose comes from

Every one of us wants to optimize ourselves along the lines of excellence. The Greeks called this happiness. And the mystery of happiness is mastery. Think about the first time you learned to ride a bicycle. You probably spent most of your time watching your feet on the pedals. But once you mastered the skill, you could enjoy the wind on your face.

But before we master performance, we have to muster *passion*—and that's where purpose comes in. Purpose creates passion, and passion sustains us on our journey to what eminent psychologist Abraham Maslow called self-actualization, becoming all you can be.

Business and its brands can self-actualize as well. And the good news is it takes a lot less time when you have a purpose. The path to purpose takes 16 weeks, and the rewards for taking this journey can last forever.

The Story Behind the Story

Beginnings hold vital instructions for the future. *Ethos* is a beginning. From here, every business is launched, every brand is created, and your corporate culture is built.

Over time, ethos attracts people with shared beliefs called *culture*. Culture is the soul or spirit of an organization. When culture is compromised, it generates corporate anxiety. Associates fear their future. Healthy culture, on the other hand, creates an atmosphere of flourishing.

Positive cultures are held together by core beliefs called *values*. These values are the pillars that hold the culture up and tell people how they should behave.

Together, ethos, culture, and values create the "black box" of *strategy*. This box informs, guides, and accelerates strategy, which is a plan of action. The strategic plan is then translated into daily *tactics*.

This is called The BrightHouse Ellipse (see Figure P.II.1), the subject of Part II, and it is the road map to a place called Camelot.

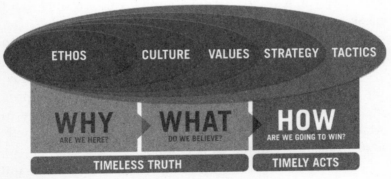

FIGURE P.II.1   The BrightHouse Ellipse

Source: © BrightHouse. Illustration by David Paprocki.

4

Ethos

The Fruits Are in the Roots

Story comes from the word history.

—Joey Reiman,
on ethos

Today, countless companies and brands are returning to their roots to find their origins of inspiration, distinctiveness, and soul. President of Cinnabon, Kat Cole, states, "The same is true for business. At Cinnabon, we believe that 'Life Needs Frosting.' We know our place in the world and the market, and we are proud of it. Our most famous products may be indulgent, but they are good for your soul. Everyone deserves a treat sometimes, and we are clear that our purpose is to help people treat themselves. We focus on our purpose, and this keeps us differentiated and on course. It helps the franchise partners stay focused and pushes them to succeed by having the clear sense of purpose and not letting it get convoluted." These are the fruits that allow them to grow and prosper while remaining guided by their true purposes.

Every organization has the potential to find remarkable power in its roots—since this is where companies and brands begin to grow. It is where their ethos, a corporation's characteristics, lies and where the core sentiment, the seed of the organization, was originally planted. Chief executive officer (CEO) of Boston Market, George Michel, remarks, "One of the lessons learned was sticking to the original Boston Chicken format—neighborhood locations with a smaller footprint as opposed to having gone to freestanding buildings with drive-thru windows. This changed the concept from fast casual to fast food." Michel continues, "A freestanding location is around 3,200 to 3,600 square feet. But, we're not entertaining freestanding locations anymore. We're going back to our roots."

Here in the roots we discover and *re*cover what makes our enterprise distinctive, powerful, and precious. We find the answer to the question, "What makes us soulful in a world of sameness?" It is in these roots that the organization's DNA resides, where its potential first blossomed, and where it possessed what I call soulful excellence—organizational vitality that radiates from its original purpose.

Too often companies, even the biggest ones, lose their way and forget what it is that made them great in the first place. Too many forget about their beginnings and don't know how to get it back. It's easy to do in a world that demands daily operational excellence. But there is a cost that comes with leaving your company's past behind and cutting your organization off from its roots. When you lose your roots, you lose your purpose and meaning. Conversely, there are rich rewards for those who reconnect with their company's origin. When you rediscover your organization's true identity—what it once stood for—you will gain fresh insight into the reasons for its existence, its essence, its *why*—that is, its very soul.

Ethos doesn't change over time. To discover what will make your company or brand truly great in the years to come is to discover its history, its *why*, and to rebuild from there.

With the global search for meaning in the twenty-first century, from corporations as well as individuals, this work is ripe for the picking. It is a road map to the way back to our roots that will produce new fruits for our labors.

Reconnecting with your business's initial, historical, and authentic thinking will fertilize, nourish, restore, and grow unprecedented emotional, intellectual, and financial revenues. An authentic purpose promises to help leaders, organizations, companies big and small, and marketers excavate the treasures that lie right beneath them.

The Power of Beginnings

The word *original* does not mean "novel" but rather "source." As such, ethos gets at the source of a brand, company, or word.

You've likely noticed by now that I reference the etymology of words to discover their original meanings. That's because the story of purpose is about excavation. We dig for answers in order to learn *why* a company or brand exists. Words and symbols hold valuable clues to the answer. That's why we use the tools of etymology and ideograms. The word *etymology* is from the Greek *etymologia*, which means "the study of the true sense of a word."[1] Ideograms are graphic symbols that represents ideas through history. Together, these instruments help us assemble pieces of a puzzle that will eventually become a Master Idea or authentic purpose.

Beginnings tell us what is special about us, our companies, and brands and what distinguished them from one another. Ethos serves as a unifier between that which was and that which can be, and it is what helps us reconcile past and future promises.

Have You Met Life Today?

The quest for our beginnings allows human beings and organizations to create the instructive stories we seek. One such story is that of the National Union Life and Limb Insurance Company, founded in 1863 by a group of businessmen from the metropolitan district called New York City. The group wanted to ensure Civil War soldiers and sailors that they would be taken care of when they got home. That assurance would become the foundation of insurance and the ethos of newly named Metropolitan Life Insurance Company.

This benevolent enterprise would soon become a household name with agents who actually visited their clients at home. They met face to face to listen to clients' problems, concerns, and hopes for the future. Assurance of a protected, productive, and happy life helped MetLife become America's largest life insurer.

After more than a century of serving the public, the privately held firm decided to go public. For this behemoth task, MetLife's board brought in CEO Robert H. Benmosche. Around this time, I met with Benmosche privately at an off-site chateau in Tarrytown, New York. We sat down at a table, and the magic began.

I arrived to take Benmosche on a journey to recover the Holy Grail of MetLife; he was there to transform MetLife into a financial juggernaut. We both saw opportunity: he saw it in the future; I saw it in the past. He was focused on shareholder value, whereas I was thinking about organizational values. At that intersection, I would find the model for building a purpose-inspired business.

The World's Wealthiest Private Company

Purpose work allows me to meet people in a company—from the top floor to factory floor. But my favorite place is often the basement, because this is where the archives rest. MetLife's archivist provides moving stories of people who were dedicated to liberating people financially so that they could live life more deeply.

During World War II, MetLife offered benefits to veterans even though they may not have held a policy with the organization. As early as 1909, MetLife announced, "Insurance is not merely a business proposition but a social program."

This policy would shape the company and guide its decisions. MetLife went on to become the primary underwriter of children's inoculation programs, as well a strong advocate of women's rights and initiatives to bring equality to the workplace. The company headquarters even served meals to their associates to show their benevolence and appreciation for playing a caring and nurturing role in people's lives.

Perhaps that is why they grew to the largest privately held company in America during the 1940s. The reason is simple: in peace or war, MetLife took orders from a higher command: *purpose*. Serving, guiding, and healing ultimately led them to build a purpose-focused organization that has endeared itself to people. And in the business of purpose, endearing is enduring.

Insuring a Whole Life

MetLife has continued to make purposeful contributions over the years by supporting war efforts, urban renewal projects, and community financing. Although it's an insurance company on the books, MetLife also promises its policyholders a life of significance off the books. The way Benmosche sees it, "If we give people financial freedom, they can fully live their lives." For a CEO to recognize that true freedom is to discover your deepest whole self is truly profound.

Inspired, we crafted the Master Idea in the form of a question: "Have you Met Life today?"

MetLife achieved its vision when it went public to again be in the major league of financial companies. It galvanized around its original purpose: to insure a life of significance. Policyholders reacted with resounding sales, and shareholders benefited from meteoric growth.

Benmosche consolidated Traveler's Life & Annuity under "his umbrella" and entered the retail banking business to further expand MetLife's reach. MetLife went on to be named Best Managed Insurance Company in 2008 and landed on *Fortune*'s list of most admired companies. Today, AIG, where Benmosche is currently CEO, is the largest insurance company in the world. But for me, MetLife will always be the first organization that had the foresight to go back to move forward.

The work that we did would serve as the foundation for the next two decades of purpose work with the best companies in the world. In a generative sense, Benmosche's company has helped hundreds of others "meet life" in a whole new way.

Return to Ethos for Greater Returns

Founded in 1932 on the principle of "leg godt," Danish for "play well," Lego has made 600 billion interlocking blocks. That's about 80 blocks for every human being on Earth. But building the company wasn't always a snap. From 1998 through 2004, the company suffered financial decline, as Lego was not the only choice on the block.

Lego tried to build back share by expanding into new business areas where families with children would be. Thus, the Lego brand endorsed clothing, watches, books, and nonconstruction toys. But expanding into new areas, even those with high potential, can lead companies away from their original ethos. In Lego's case, the company was moving away from classic building. And returning to one's ethos can be the missing piece to a comeback.

In 2005, Lego returned to its roots by making new versions of original toys such as Castle and City that teach children how to build their imaginations. Lego also divested itself of anything that was not related to their core business: toys. The company licensed video games to its partners and sold its theme parks.

Most inspiring, though, was how Lego used its earliest principle of *play well* to rebuild their own organization. By tearing down silos, having teams collaborate across functions, and working more closely with important stakeholders such as the retailer, Lego was able to play well in the world again.

In 2009, Lego's net profit reached 2,204 million Danish Krone (Denmark's currency)—approximately 372 million US dollars. This is an increase of 71 percent since it returned to its origin in 2006. With just six 2×4 Legos, you can create 9,103,765 combinations, but the foundational block of ethos is how Lego inspired a whole new generation to build their imaginations.

We Exist versus We Discover

When I was first asked to help Procter & Gamble build their new purpose marketing framework, company executives showed me an existing model that asked the brand team to begin with the words "We exist to ..." Those words were followed by, "therefore" and "we will." All activities of the brand would then emanate from "We exist to ..."

I will share the same note of caution with you that I shared with some of the best marketing minds in Cincinnati: people don't merely *exist*. Therefore, neither do brands and companies. The word *corporation* actually derives from *corpus*, the Latin word for "body."[2] And like our bodies, organizations exist for a reason, which we create when we discover something meaningful.

By instead beginning with the words "We *discover*," our purpose journey becomes more authentic and our outcome more grand. Take Newell Rubbermaid's Calphalon brand as an example.

I was first introduced to Calphalon's president, Kristie Juster at the time, after she had watched a purpose film we had created for Calphalon's sister brand and infant goods manufacturer Graco. From the back of the auditorium, she jumped up and proclaimed, "I want to do this for *my* business!"

Often, purpose takes on the tenor of a religious revival; we reawaken something sacred when we discover ethos. Up until that point, Calphalon, like so many brands, was built by developing a strategy based on the product benefits and the market research. Then, in edict fashion, a strategy brief was handed down that told marketers and their partners, "We exist to ..."

Discovery of an organization's ethos changed this outdated process. By going back to the beginning of the story, we can better predict the next chapter for our business. The story of Calphalon starts with a hero named Ron Kasperzak. He was not only the founder of Calphalon cookware but America's original bon vivant. He was cooking up a storm in Ohio way before *The Galloping Gourmet* came onto the scene. He, along with Chuck Sonoma of Williams-Sonoma, Julia Child, and others, launched the culinary movement in the United States.

Discovering this ethos led Juster to rethink Calphalon's offerings. Her conclusion was not cookware but an entire lifestyle. Sharing meals was Kasperzak's life and also the recipe for Calphalon's success.

Juster had all the ingredients for success—a delicious story, a team that was cooking, rediscovered values to serve up, and a new strategy. She was not selling pots and pans; she was continuing Kasperzak's culinary movement that made the company so hot in the first place.

After this revelation, our purpose team articulated the Master Idea: "Shared Is the Appetite for Life."

Discovering this Master Idea led Juster to rethink Calphalon's offerings, expanding into near-neighbor categories such as culinary accessories, cutlery, and even electric gadgets. Calphalon sold not just for cookware but the whole cooking lifestyle. This was reflected in the brand's office space as well: the corporate headquarters, which had been a "pots and pans" ninth floor, became a supercharged kitchen that the brand team had installed. They were cooking up new products and services that helped people share food and conversations around the table and the world.

Beginning with discovery had led the team to now say "They exist" for an authentic reason. Discovering Calphalon's ethos had made an otherwise flavorless process delicious.

Visit Your Archivist Today

Fruitful companies and brands go back to their roots to discover their beginnings—and your organization is no different. You can do the same by talking to the gardeners who nurtured your organization when it was a seedling. Visit your archivist. As far as I'm concerned, the archivist is the new superhero in your organization. Archivists are the keepers of ethos and history. Yours will help you tell your story.

In fact, the word *history* is from the Latin *historia*, which means "story."[3]

Their archives are treasures troves filled with stories to inspire and guide your organization. Phil Mooney, The Coca-Cola Company's chief archivist, believes that his company's future is in its history. "Going back to our roots gives us permission to believe and act like much more than a soft drink. We can once again become a symbol of good."

Ethos is part of the secret formula of purpose. As we will learn in Chapter 5, it is the foundation for building your corporate culture and bringing you closer to Camelot.

What Is the Purpose of This Chapter?

- Our roots hold the answers to what makes our enterprise distinctive, powerful, and precious.
- Reconnecting with your business's authentic purpose will nourish, restore, and grow unprecedented emotional, intellectual, and financial revenues.
- By going back to the beginning of the story, you can better predict the next chapter for your business.

Purpose Pointers

- Be an archeologist and excavate your ethos.
- Buy your archivist lunch.
- Celebrate your past, and you will celebrate in the future.

5

Culture

Creating the Cult in Your Culture

Culture is not what you do, but what you have done.

—Joey Reiman,
on culture

I love my morning yogurt. The culture that grew it makes me feel healthy and ready to take on the day. Culture works the same way in organizations. When it is active and alive, it makes your day. It's what gets you up in the morning. *Culture creates aliveness.*

Culture is composed of an organization's shared beliefs. When those beliefs are aligned but not intense, malaise develops in the company. When the shared beliefs are misaligned and intense, disagreement brews. Only when beliefs are aligned and intense does a strong belief system develop.

Different companies have a variety of different qualities that underlie their culture. But all successful companies have a strong culture. For instance, Hyundai offers customers the WALKAWAY Program, which allows consumers to return their Hyundai if they lose their income and cannot make the car payments.[1] *Compassion* is their culture. Organic grocer Whole Foods Market counts the planet as a stakeholder. John Mackey is the chief executive officer (CEO), but his company's culture reports in to Mother Nature. In this way, *culture creates stories*.

The Stories of Newell Rubbermaid

The 14 stories of the Newell Rubbermaid headquarters building in Atlanta, Georgia, tell of each of the many brands' cultures. The elevator ride takes you on a trip through what Newell Rubbermaid calls "Brands That Matter." Nearly all the company's key brands have taken journeys to find their purpose. And in 2011, the company went on the journey to discover and articulate its corporate Master Idea: "Helping people to flourish."

The floor with hair accessories brand Goody espouses the purpose that "Confidence becomes you." Mirrors, antique comb sets, and framed letters share tales of Goody brushes, clips, and elastics adorned by three generations. Goody says that their recent acquisition of Solano hair dryers was made possible only because the Solano family supported the idea that this was the right cultural fit. Turn the corner and you will find the brand's timeline, history, and walls displaying quotes from their founders and fans.

The next stop is the floor for culinary brand Calphalon; here retail customer partners cook together at a full-service commercial kitchen to experience new products. The Décor floor, which consists of home window fashion brand Levolor and decorative hardware designer Amerock, feels more like a chic home than the business unit of a nearly

$6 billion company that sells its brands in more than 90 countries.

The elevator doors open once again on baby and parenting brand Graco's floor, where associates can take a stroll through the brand's history while clients are nurtured with their Master Idea: "Cradle those who cradle them."

Purpose-inspired interiors are demonstrable ways of reflecting and expressing corporate and brand culture, because they start where culture is most important—on the inside. This is not about companies living in the past, but recognizing the past lives that live in them today.

When BrightHouse excavates a company's purpose, we create a 3-minute purpose film that tells the story of the company and why it is here. Each movie has a soundtrack that captures the rhythm and theme of the company. These are not advertising jingles; rather, they're corporate anthems.

Culture Begins at Home

How does your company build culture? Culture is not something you do, but rather something you *did*. It is shaped by the events that those who came before us shared and experienced. When we join a culture, we are the new characters in that story. So what will your character contribute?

There's a legendary tale of the day a man walked into The Home Depot with a tire on his shoulder. When he tells an associate he needs to return the tire, the associate starts to question him, but a store manager interrupts and asks him how much he paid for it. The man responds and the manager opens a register, pulls out a handful of bills, and gives him the full amount in cash. As the man leaves, the store manager turns and hangs the tire on the wall. For years, it hangs as a symbol of the culture on which the company—*which has never sold tires*—was built.

The Home Depot's CEO Frank Blake comments that at a 2007 store manager meeting of thousands of associates, he gave out a golden tire. "One of the key values that drives our culture is 'doing the right thing.' This is symbolized by that golden tire."

Symbols of Great Culture

What's your company's symbol? What does it stand for? Does it inspire you? Would you wear it on a T-shirt, a bag, or a baseball cap? The Greeks interpreted the word *symbolon* to mean "throw things together"[2]; in their time, that meant a little of heaven and a little of Earth. Today, great corporate symbols do the same. The signature swoosh tells us it's Nike, but it is also imbued with the idea of performance. Mickey Mouse ears say Disney as well as magic, and the iconic apple says computer—but at its core, creativity.

The Best Culture Not on Earth

Southwest Airlines is often cited as a company with great purpose: to democratize the skies. Actually, the idea is not new. Juan Trippe, founder of both Pan American World Airways and what was a division of Pan Am, the Intercontinental Hotels, believed that humans have an inalienable right to travel. So in the 1970s, Trippe introduced lower fares on many of the company's routes. Pan Am's new class was called the rainbow. Customers flew in smaller seats with a five-across layout instead of the four-across offered in first class. The idea is now called coach class.[3]

What is new is Southwest Airlines' fanatical focus on culture as a platform for growth. Ever since Southwest Airlines took off from Love Field in Dallas, Texas, in 1971, it has become an expert in the field of love.[4] Southwest's workforce is more of a lovefest. Weekly deck parties and chili cook-offs for new hires are the ingredients for this high-flying culture. When Southwest Airlines created a hub in Atlanta, Georgia, 4,500 Southwest associates showed up for a company rally.

In a conversation with Ginger Hardage, senior vice president of culture and communications, she shared with me that "95 percent of employees are proud to work for Southwest Airlines. [So] important is culture at Southwest, the company created a culture club to keep the inspiration going and growing."

Employees truly do "Live the Southwest Way," when they participate wholeheartedly in the company's culture. Operation: Kick Tail uses Kick Tail-A-Grams to recognize outstanding performance "on the spot," says Hardage. "With almost 90 percent employee participation, we give back $1 million in cash and prizes if certain performance goals are met. Employees feel proud of their efforts and understand that the larger team is proud of them too. This takes Southwest's employee engagement up in altitude—thousands of feet."

How powerful can company culture be? Just tune in to the new TV show *On the Fly* on TLC. It's all about Southwest Airlines and their culture. And it's a reality show. If your culture were a TV show, would it be a comedy, an action-adventure, a low-budget Indie, a romance, or a tragedy? Great cultures are produced and directed by the people who act in them every day.

When Culture Is Grounded

The tale of Delta Air Lines is one about the world's most revered airline and how it remembers how to fly through culture.

There has never been a more troubled period in aviation history than the year 2002. Planes that were empty thanks to post-9/11 fear of air travel, rising fuel costs, and a downward-spiraling economy created a turbulent industry. Delta was bleeding $120 million a month, and employee morale was grounded. And although company leaders might have assumed this would not be the best time to focus on culture, they realized that purpose sustains culture in the worst of times and elevates it in the best of times.

I turn now to Delta's flight plan to kick-start a 747. I know of no other company facing Chapter 11 Bankruptcy that looked to another chapter in their culture for instruction. Delta Air Lines sets its coordinates for Monroe, Louisiana, 1929, where founder C. E. Woolman began to build a company he hoped would do more than move people from one point to another. Woolman wanted to lift them emotionally as well.

Taking Culture to Heart

We learned when we focused on purpose—that is, when we developed a Master Idea—with Delta that Woolman's hard work ethic and down-to-Earth demeanor, instilled in him since childhood, allowed him to run a company that focused on always putting the customer first. Delta remembers that he would often say, "Let's put ourselves on the other side of the counter." Woolman knew that attitude is more important than altitude. He played piano on the tarmac as his planes took off, personally pinning wings and orchids on flight attendants and spending many late nights sitting atop oil drums talking aviation with his mechanics. Woolman kept every letter sent to him by employees.

Under Woolman's watch, employees treated passengers as exalted guests. A ticket guaranteed pampering, politeness, and respect, and the gray flannel cabin was elegant and stylish, welcoming the dapper and the delicate. Attention to detail was found in the spray of a lemon zest across the rim of an icy martini and the sprig of rosemary gently tucked into a roasted Georgia mountain trout. For Delta Air Lines, the best table was in the air.

Flying Again on Purpose

As a counselor and passenger on Delta's purpose journey, it was easy to see a future for Delta by studying its past. Back then, the crew created a culture that told us—the passengers—how to fly. Woolman saw flight as a memorable experience that could lift all our senses. Culturally, the nascent airline was creating the story of flight: its grandeur and promise.

Yet by 2002, Delta had departed from its origins. It was untethered to its culture and utterly lost. Once unearthed, its culture could rise again. Delta's purpose team worked for months to recover the company's ethos of hospitality and heart, its culture of aliveness and style, and its values of serving passengers and the world.

Four thousand Delta associates gathered in Hangar One in Atlanta, Georgia, one summer morning in 2003. The Master Idea, "Lift the world," was presented with a sermon-like passion. A gospel choir swayed as it sang the "Lift the world" anthem. Then the lights dimmed, and a film flickered on-screen showing Delta Air Lines bringing the Master Idea to life and bringing thousands to their feet. Mechanics, pilots, flight attendants, and reservation clerks are crying, laughing, and holding and hugging one another as though they've found salvation. And a new era began.

The premise of *The Story of Purpose* is that ethos—the original character of the company—put forth by C. E. Woolman can be reinstated at any time by leadership. More than a decade ago, Delta Air Lines reconnected with its purpose, and today we can watch Delta's in-flight video of CEO Richard Anderson standing behind Woolman's desk recalling the founder's values. That is a high-flying lesson for business. Whether you say, "Lift the world" or "Keep Climbing," we are inspired by the man who played piano for his company and passengers on the tarmac almost a century ago.

How Will You Lift the World?

Culture carries its weight. One that is as strong as Delta's can lift a whole world. To build great corporate cultures, we need lots of people aligned around strong beliefs. What do you and the other members of your organization feel strongest about? Does your company amplify your beliefs or make you feel like you have to bury them?

I have worked in numerous corporate cultures throughout the world and have found that the best are filled with people who are free to be their authentic selves and who are accountable to something greater than just wealth creation and shareholder value. Lift your world by becoming more of *who you are* at work. Then, together with others, put your shared beliefs to work on behalf of something greater. When a culture does that, they get religion.

Culture Is Religion

The world's greatest brands have been in business for more than 3,000 years. They are global, and together they have more than 12 million locations. Each has a logo that people worship, even die for, and thousands of new customers sign up every minute. The people who work for these organizations love their boss. Of course, I am talking about religion. And the boss is "something greater."

The word *religion* is from the Latin *relegare*, which means "to bind fast to or to go through again"[5]—which is exactly what culture does. The Golden Rule is also central to all religious dogma. Great corporate cultures have many of the same qualities as religion. The best corporate cultures don't "do like others"; they "do *unto* others."

"There's a spiritual aspect to business. Most people would agree that there's a spiritual part of our lives as individuals,"[6] writes purposeful leader Jerry Greenfield, cofounder of Ben & Jerry's Ice Cream. Cofounder Ben Cohen adds, "As you give, you receive, as you help others you are helped in return, as your business supports the community, the community supports your business."[7]

Faced with the Great Depression of 1929, Milton Hershey's chief operating officer (COO) purchased five machines from Germany that could each do the work of 100 men. It makes sense to replace men with machines that did not demand wages, right? Wrong, said Milton. When learning of this, he had the machines returned immediately and instructed his COO to hire even more men.

Replacement was not an option for Milton Hershey. Not even a boost in productivity could erase the importance of people and culture in Hershey's company. This was—and still is—an organization committed to fostering a healthy and supportive culture for its workers, inside the factory as well as outside.

Hershey provided all sorts of benefits, including education opportunities, that he was not given as a young man. Hershey built a community with housing for executives and workers, as well as schools, churches, parks, transportation, and recreation opportunities.

According to the Hershey Company, "He believed that workers who were treated fairly and who lived in a comfortable, pleasant environment would be better workers. Accordingly, he set upon building an infrastructure to take care of the people who were employed by his company." Hershey is a role model for purposeful culture.[8]

Sun Capital Capitalizes on Culture

When co-CEOs Rodger Krouse and Marc Leder started private equity firm Sun Capital Partners, Inc., in 1995, they were 33 years old—fresh from fact-based, numbers-based, results-driven Lehman Brothers. Neither man was focused on culture, which doesn't come as much of a surprise. So you can imagine my own when I learned that one of the world's largest and most prestigious private equity firms relies on culture for its success. Typically, private equity firms make investments in its operating companies through a variety of strategies, including leveraged buyout, venture capital, and growth capital. Very rarely does this include culture.

"Culture is our strategy at Sun Capital," Krouse tells me. "Our revelation came in 2008, when all our companies were hit hard and we saw [that those] with strong cultures had the best financial results." Krouse continues, "The Limited [clothing chain] stores had been losing lots of money for 17 years when we bought it. The first place we focused on was its culture. Core values are very important, and leaders need to practice what they preach. Ignoring core values can get you in trouble."

Culture Fixes What Is Broken

Krouse continues to say that they see a lot of broken culture in these broken companies: "Businesses are a collection of assets ... *and* people. Unify them with a common purpose, and you get excellence." Sun Capital purchases companies that are broke and losing money. Executives know that the only way to truly "fix" the companies is to unify the people. "We are doing what many people would think is statistically impossible. But you can achieve it if you have a great culture," Krouse explains.

One of the keys in improving culture is communication—which is frequent and transparent. People feel a lot better about the organization when they know the truth about what's going on and hear about it often. They feel that the organization cares about them when people communicate with them. The more people understand what you are trying to achieve as a company, the more people can pitch in. Culture is constancy.

Krouse attributes the successful relaunches of Boston Market and Captain D's, which had both been skidding for years, to highly engaged people on a common mission.

When you meet Boston Market CEO George Michel, he will be wearing a Boston Market apron to match his staff of 15,000 employees. And don't call him Mr. Michel either. He would rather be addressed by the title on his business card: "The Big Chicken" (Figure 5.1).

FIGURE 5.1   George Michel's Business Card
Source: Boston Market Corporation.

Beloved by everyone from his crew to CNN's Anderson Cooper—who dines at his restaurants often—Michel rules his roost by focusing on culture. "It begins with MBWA—Management By Wandering Around," Michel tells me. "Observation leads to education, and that leads to success." This concept must have worked, as sales are up nearly 10 percent since he arrived.

"It's all about the puck in the net." George gives out hockey pucks to people who stand out. Recently, he upped his game by giving personally autographed hockey sticks from the Florida Panthers to those who reached their financial goals.

The Big Chicken proves that a company's culture—like a sports team—needs a captain that employees can look up to. Recently, Anderson Cooper invited Michel to his show, saying, "George, meeting you is like meeting Santa Claus for the first time." I have to agree. Twenty-four hours after interviewing The Big Chicken, I received Boston Market gift cards. It's part of their culture—and Boston Market is part of mine.

The "D" in restaurant chain Captain D's stands for founder Ray Danner, but for Phil Greifeld, CEO of Captain D's, the "D" stands for "discretionary effort." "That's the extra effort someone will make to take care of the guests," says Greifeld.

Captain D's, a US fast food chain that specializes in seafood, fish, and chips, almost sank after losing money for nearly a decade. "This was a brand without purpose, without leadership, and clearly without a culture. People came to work [at] a mind-numbing job where there was no direction, and no one knew what was expected of them," Greifeld tells me. "Today, we have instilled strong values. We are an organization that treats people with respect and genuine care and that's paid off."

A recent culture survey that Captain D's uses for all its employees was off the charts in many areas, especially the one that Phil is most proud of: "I love what I do," which scored a 90 percent in terms of emotional connection. Fiscal year 2011 was the first year in nine years that the company produced positive sales growth. "Our 2012 comps almost makes us the leader in the entire restaurant industry," boasts Greifeld.

Boston Market and Captain D's are two examples in a portfolio of world-renowned brands that includes The Limited and American Standard, organizations where the real private equity is culture. For its part, Sun Capital has invested in more than 300 companies worldwide since 1995, with combined sales in excess of $45 billion. According to Krouse, "We have better returns because we have high performance cultures across the portfolio companies."

One of Ben & Jerry's flavors is called "Everything but the … ," and as you can imagine, it's got everything in it. Culture works the same way. When "everything but" goes into a culture, the result is more engaged people. What we

think of as human resources becomes human resourceful-
ness as employees employ their full selves in service of the
organization, its community, and the world. Great culture
respects its greatest asset: its people. *Respect* comes from
the Latin word *respectus*, meaning *treat with deferential regard
or esteem.*[9] People give culture its distinct flavor.

What Is the Purpose of This Chapter?

- Culture is defined by an organization's shared beliefs.
- Culture is what makes a company come alive.
- Associates aligned around a common purpose create
  advocacy.

Purpose Pointers

- Be a character in your company's story.
- Feed the culture to keep it alive.
- Culture thrives on shared beliefs.

6

Values

Your Most Valuable Asset

Values are the language of an organization.

—Joey Reiman,
on Values

In 1993, a young maverick named Charles Brewer pinned up a set of core values for his budding Internet company, MindSpring, on the wall of his apartment in Atlanta. Those values, which included frugality, respect for the individual, and the notion that work should be fun, were upheld to the day MindSpring merged with EarthLink in 2000 and became an estimated $4 billion telecommunications giant.

What's truly remarkable is that Brewer had no idea what business he would start when he identified his company's core values. "I thought there had to be a way to do things [and treat] customers better," he told me. "The only way to be different was to focus on the values. I wrote them down ahead of time, several months before I determined the business." Laughing, Brewer says he had to start a business eventually because "the values were not generating profits on their own."

Why Values Count

"If ethics are rules, then values are guides. And they're hot today. Values are on everyone's mind," says Philip Kotler, renowned marketing expert and professor at Northwestern University's Kellogg School of Management.

But values haven't always been in the forefront of business. Kotler believes this emerging values revolution comes on the heels of unprecedented corporate corruption and public disillusionment. "This is the result of our obsession with materialism at the expense of values such as friendship and community," he says, pointing to "certain companies' greedy behavior, their abuse of customer trust, and people in power paying themselves huge salaries."

In the 1980s, often called the Age of Greed, hostile takeovers were common. Even motion pictures portrayed ruthless corporate traders as heroes (for example, Gordon Gekko in the 1987 movie *Wall Street*).

It might seem to some that values have taken a beating lately. Politicians seem most interested in serving their own interests first, while athletes use steroids to win and business barons appear willing to do anything to make their fortunes last. However, I have seen plenty of instances in the past decade of leaders and companies putting values *first*. Good values are the new bosses. And when organizational leaders don't merely hang them on a wall but authentically speak them—when they don't just print them on the backs of business cards, but adhere to them—then they truly come to life. Values create highly enthusiastic workers, dramatic profits, and legendary reputations for your business.

What Are Your Values?

No other corporate asset tells you more about what an organization values than its own values. That's why the first question I ask when meeting a company's leadership is, "What are your values?"

I generally hear three kinds of answers:

1. **Compliant values that change nothing:** These boilerplate, pabulum principles are usually found on posters and are instituted as a compliance measure to illustrate good citizenship. Unfortunately, they say little about the organization, and hence have little or no effect on its people. *Quality, teamwork, and integrity* win the day.

2. **Committed values that change your company:** These reflect the interest of the company but are limited to the organization. They tell you what the company expects *from* you but not how you might help others. Rather than a means to an end, they are ends like *be the leader* and *create shareholder value*.

3. **Influential values that change the world:** These are values that positively alter how we live and work, affecting all stakeholders—owners, employees, partners, community, and the planet. These values release human energies and liberate us to bring our whole selves to work. The best influential values have three characteristics:

   a. **Industry specific:** An example is SunTrust Bank's value: "Warmth is our currency."

   b. **Memorable:** An example is FedEx Office's value: "Turn Ideas into I Did Its."

   c. **Directive:** An example is Zappos' value to "Deliver WOW Through Service."[1]

Following are two companies that have incorporated *influential* values into their cultures. Both organizations use values to positively influence their people and society. They demonstrate through these values how business can put the moral code behind a bar code.

The Happy Meal Revolution

McDonald's did things a bit different in 2009, when they spent the year trying to improve their business of family and kids in the United States. Not only were customers considering other choices, but fast food in and of itself had started to be questioned more frequently by parents as a good nutrition option for their families. When I gave a keynote speech to McDonald's Asian leadership in Bali, Indonesia, I learned news of a further downturn. After the conference, I reached out to US chief marketing officer Neil Golden, who agreed to dine with me in Atlanta.

Throughout our meal we discussed the informal eating out category. Golden was hungry for a solution. Charged with strengthening his brand to its rightful place in the minds and stomachs of America, Golden grilled me on the benefits of purpose and whether this approach could help McDonald's improve performance to even higher levels. Conventional marketing would have Golden serve up everyday value, a good-quality product, and a comfortable restaurant. But Golden knew that he needed more than a menu fix for the Happy Meal; he needed a revolution.

When you meet Neil Golden, you are immediately struck by how fit he is. Golden works out seven days a week for at least an hour a day. And you might also be surprised to learn that he also eats McDonald's every day: "My favorite meal is a Big Mac, Southwest Salad, and a Mango Pineapple smoothie."

Just joining McDonald's after working at a competitor, Golden and I talked about his first week on the job, a story that paints a picture of McDonald's culture. While staying in an Indianapolis hotel, he received a call from his boss, who invited the young marketing supervisor to go to the new Ronald McDonald House in Indianapolis. The president of McDonald's was going to be there to help dedicate it.

Golden suited up and arrived at the House. McDonald's president reached out to shake his hand but never got to it. Instead, he pulled out a pen with a competitor's logo on it from Golden's shirt pocket. The president accompanied Golden and his boss to a construction person on-site, who crushed the pen with pliers. "Buy a pen with the McDonald's logo on it so you know where you are and who loves you. And send me the receipt." More than 20 years later, Golden still has the McDonald's Cross pen—and it is a prized possession.

From Toys to Joys

In taking the journey to discover the purpose of McDonald's USA, Golden put his brand strategy on full stop until the "black box" of ethos, culture, and values were explored. The journey took 16 weeks, covered 50 years of culture, and involved dozens of interviews—beginning with cofounder Fred Turner's golden insight on McDonald's ethos of jazz that we discussed in Chapter 1.

After my interview with Turner, I headed back to BrightHouse to learn that the team had 71 interviews lined up at McDonald's. Although this might sound exhaustive, purpose demands a rich cross section of inputs—and the deeper we dug, the greater the treasure we'd find.

McDonald's was once the enabler of joys rather than a destination for toys. A simple roadside concept that offered a burger, fries, and shake to a world that had taken to the road was a big surprise in the 1950s. But that surprise was gone now—and so went the joy. "The treat is good, but there is an aspect of joy that was missing. And we felt that we needed to reenergize the joy part of the equation," says Golden. Conclusion: get back to joy.

Three months into the project the team landed on McDonald's purpose for kids and families in the United States: "Fill Families with Joy."

WWKD (What Would Kroc Do?)

Although the Master Idea of serving families was heralded at McDonald's headquarters, it was the values that would change the way that they would do business. When the project started, BrightHouse received a list of McDonald's values: quality, optimism, passion, and teamwork, including about five others.

"These are the values our parents teach us. What about the ones founder Ray Kroc had us learn?" I asked. What might have been a fireable moment ignited a spark in the room that blazed a way back to McDonald's ethos and a memorable set of values. If you can't recite your values, forget about them. The language of values should be rich in ethos, authentic, and fun to say.

So what were the "Krocisms"? What would Kroc do? The team presented these new (old) values to a room of nearly 100 McDonald's associates. While sitting there, I received an e-mail from Golden, who was seated at the head of the table. It read: "Home Run."

Today, the following values serve as guideposts for McDonald's USA associates and franchises. As great values do, they lay out a company's or brand's principles that influence behavior and amplify the organization's purpose.

Your company's values serve these key purposes:

1. Help you recruit and select new associates
2. Direct training and onboarding of new employees

3. Serve as guidelines for decision making
4. Drive communications internally and externally
5. Inform policies, incentives, and reward systems

The McDonald's Values

Ketchup in Their Veins

There may be no other company that earns the kind of loyalty, energy, or excitement from its employees than McDonald's does. Starting at the organization's roots, leaders like Ray Kroc, Fred Turner, and Paul Schrage lived and breathed this aliveness. From the fry cooks who become owners/operators, to grill men who become executives, their people have a passion that extends into every waking and sleeping moment of their lives.

Seeing the Milkshake as Half Full

Fifty-two-year-old Ray Kroc used his off-the-chart confidence to make his dream come true.

His long-held belief that each person makes his or her own happiness gave Kroc the optimistic conviction to see opportunity in the burger business and put his last dime and all his energy into building McDonald's. Although he faced numerous challenges, including several buyouts, the "great french-fry flop," and keeping one business alive through the income of another, Kroc learned from each experience, always sure he would succeed.

One in a Billion

Members of the McFamily may go into business for themselves, but they are never *by* themselves. They consider themselves to be thousands serving billions. Kroc recognized the possibility of McDonald's when he saw the value of his relationship with the franchisees. He saw McDonald's as "an organization of small businessmen." In his eyes, it was very similar to his first love: jazz. Kroc insisted that even though McDonald's was a large group, its soloists be given the freedom to play a role in society.

Drive Through It

Out of Kroc's depression-era Midwestern roots came his conviction in the value of a hard day's work. "Luck is the dividend of sweat," he would say. Kroc was never too proud to grab a mop and help the janitor clean restrooms, even if he was wearing his best suit. As a "doing company," all McDonald's employees, from grill man to chief executive officer (CEO), measure their achievement by their effort. Creating memorable customer experiences may not be rocket science, but they take burgers more seriously than anyone else does. And the profits this effort brings are never won merely by luck.

The Golden (Arches) Rule

Employees at McDonald's do the right thing, not the easy thing. In the very beginning, Kroc's dealings with the McDonald brothers laid this solid moral ground. To this day, we honor Kroc's straight shooting sense of integrity in all we do, including going into the community and giving back through our unspoken efforts. From the Ronald McDonald House Charities to sponsoring countless children's sports teams, we do the right thing. Always.

How Will We Fill Families with Joy?

"That's the most important question I ask myself as I review ideas to build the business and brand," says Golden. "The question keeps our purpose front and center daily." As for tomorrow, "When I look ahead, I look to the things we need to do to continue to bring joy." He tells me that by the printing of this book, McDonald's will introduce an initiative they call Favorites Under 400. This program will highlight more than 40 different menu items that are all less than 400 calories; approximately 80 percent of McDonald's entire menu falls within 400 calories.

Adding fruit to every Happy Meal means McDonald's gives children the nourishment parents love as well. What's more, every Happy Meal sold at participating McDonald's restaurants comes with the promise that a penny goes to the Ronald McDonald House to help others in need.

By serving up their original purpose and values, McDonald's has posted remarkable results. Filled with joy, Golden shares with me that "McDonald's visitation, sales, market share, and restaurant cash flow are at all-time highs."

Kevin Newell, global brand chief of McDonald's, wrote to me, "To thine own self be true. It works on a personal level as well as for brands."

BrightHouse Values

We use the lens of purpose to turn compliant generic values into dynamic authentic language. Once completed, everyone within the organization not only knows the values, they live them. We further assign icons to our values (Figure 6.1). From the Greek word for *image*, an icon is a religious work of art meant to inspire and teach.

THE BEAUTY OF ELOQUENCE   FAMILY IS EVERYTHING   LIGHTING THE WAY   FROM WONDER? TO WONDER!   INTELLIGENCE HAVING FUN

FIGURE 6.1   BrightHouse Values

Source: © BrightHouse. Illustration by David Paprocki.

The best organizations are built on strong values that influence associates every day. BrightHouse thinkers don't report in to me but to a higher office—those of the values listed here:

- **The beauty of eloquence:** We master ideas—and words and pictures. We believe communication is a craft and that if something is worth saying, it's worth saying well, because an idea without the right words is like good intentions without action. When working on FedEx Office's Master Idea we learned that one of the company's qualities was to make things happen for its customers, to "Turn Ideas into I Did Its."

- **Family is everything:** Our family begins with our husbands and wives, children, and parents and extends to our BrightHouse family, our clients, our community, and the family of all living things. Family is the most important thing. It is, indeed, *everything*. That is why I coined the term *famillionaire*, a person whose wealth is his or her family and friends. Holiday parties include not only the children of BrightHouse thinkers but our parents as well.

- **Light the way:** We strive to lead our clients with new ways of thinking and working that will create better brands and brighter companies. Come into our building and you will see a quote from Gauguin that reads 6 feet across the wall: "There are only two kinds of artists—revolutionaries and plagiarists." We live to be agents of change.

- **From Wonder? To Wonder!** Some would say that curiosity and innocence are child-like traits. We say they are the key ingredients for learning and discovery, for revelation and awe. It is our path from questioning to astonishing that creates the answers for our clients. Graco's purpose helps parents go from wonder? to wonder!

- **Creativity is intelligence having fun:** This quote from Albert Einstein brings together both sides of the brain, both sides of BrightHouse—creative and strategic. And when they come together, work is play. Companies underestimate the value of having fun. Those that bake it into their culture, like BrightHouse, Zappos, and Southwest Airlines, are smarter and richer for it.

Take another look at your values. What actions are they inspiring? Are they unique and distinctive? Do people value them? Do they sit above the leadership? Are they directive? Many organizations would fare better with *a board of directives* than with a board of directors.

The Value of Values

In the daily struggle of value versus values, many companies forsake their own ideals to deliver more bang to the bottom line. Some will even cross the line for profit.

But Philip Kotler encourages companies to put out public statements on the ideals they're passionate about: "These companies should use their values in recruiting employees and in dealing with customers, dealers, and suppliers. Companies should be ready to expose lapses and enforce their values."

Values are assets. Lived every day, they have the ability to guide us and inspire us as well as others. If purpose is the general, values are the troop. They steady companies during turbulent times and plot the best course in good times.

Like all revolutions, the movement toward values in corporate America captures more than minds and hearts. It liberates companies and people to occupy something bigger than Wall Street: their souls.

Quick, Name Your Values

If you can't count off your company's values, they don't count. And if you can list them but don't live them, you are no better off. Values without positive action to support them are meaningless.

But a company can't simply identify values that sound good. Think of BP's line, "beyond petroleum." "Values need to be authentic," Brewer says. "It's not going to work if the values aren't really important to you." So important were they to Brewer that he resigned from EarthLink because of company culture disagreements.

In Chapters 7 and 8, we will see how the black box elements of ethos, culture, and values impact and inform strategy and tactics to align and inspire organizations. As Richard Makadok, associate professor at Emory University, says, "Half a century ago, business historian Alfred Chandler revolutionized the field of management by discovering that, in every corporate reorganization, structure follows strategy. What might be even more important is the deeper realization that strategy, in turn, must follow purpose. Purpose is the 'black box' of strategy."

What Is the Purpose of This Chapter?

- Values are industry specific, memorable, and directive.
- Values create highly enthusiastic workers, dramatic profits, and legendary reputations for your business.
- Authentic values are influential, not compliant.

Purpose Pointers

- Values must be lived.
- Values provide guardrails, not guidelines.
- Create icons for your values.

7

Strategy

The Plan to Win

Why is not a question, it's the answer.

—Joey Reiman,
on how strategy is developed

Ask a hundred strategists where strategy comes from, and you will get a hundred answers. I am no different, but my colleagues in academia think I am onto something. The difference that I provide in how I built my company remains the core of how purpose is built. Purpose gives you *direction*. Strategy gives you the *directions*.

Strategy is your road map, a GPS for a company's destination in the marketplace and its destiny in the world. Strategy is essentially how to get where purpose has taken you.

Consider this explanation from Northwestern University's Kellogg School of Management professor Philip Kotler of my company BrightHouse: "Many businesses today resemble a boat lost at sea. The few that make it to shore follow the light coming from a bright idea. BrightHouse has a superb process to guide companies to their destination."

Although this quote certainly was music to my ears, we at BrightHouse consider purpose work a responsibility. It is our daily challenge to help ensure that companies effectively execute their business strategies supported by this purpose. Well-defined strategy is a lantern for your purpose expedition. Ethos, culture, and values have revealed your timeless truth—and now strategy will light the way with a timely plan. Purpose is your *why*. Strategy is your *how*. That's why if purpose is missing, your strategy is sure to miss as well.

Taking Aim to Reach the Destination

Over the past three decades, I have seen brilliant businesses fail, pricing strategies fall short, luxury strategies executed poorly, and niche strategies fail to hit their targets. The reason for breakdown was clear in all these cases: greater purpose was not the aim. If your business strategy is to get more *whats* to more *whos*, you must ask *why*.

Take the concept of war, for example. *Strategy* is a military word from the Greek word *strategia*, meaning "office of the general."[1] Wars are not won because of speed, agility, maneuverability, adaptability, or weaponry; they're won because of the sense of greater meaning that countries and armies have instilled within their soldiers. Some of the worst battles have been fought in the name of faith, religions' word for purpose. The bottom line is simple: emotion in motion wins the day.

The *why* prevails over what we have, who we are, where we are going, or how we are going to get there. Today, *why* leads the way. Procter & Gamble (P&G) has recently adopted this model for all its brands by putting a *why* before *what* and *who*. P&G's *what* is its brands; its *who* is its consumers, and its *why* is that nothing is more powerful than helping people realize their full potential so that they can thrive. To quote a P&G employee in Pakistan, "Procter & Gamble's Safeguard brand and Save the Children announced their new partnership to reach 100 primary schools in Pakistan through a school health and hygiene project. The project will benefit 40,000 school-age children in Quetta, Karachi, and Lahore with improved sanitation facilities and health and hygiene education."

All these aspects of business are changing. The *who* is changing; people want more meaning from their brands. The *what* is changing, in that products alone aren't enough; people demand service as well. The *where* is changing; digital communities are becoming larger stores. The *when* is changing from prime time to *all the time*. And the *how* is changing from monologues to dialogues. The only thing that has not changed—that will *never* change—is the *why*. *Why* is the oldest question for humankind and the newest answer for business. When we work on *why*, we get a wow.

The WOW Strategy: Work On Why

A wow moment occurs when we experience something unexpected—a baby's first step, a meteor, or a sunset—then instantly understand how it is part of something greater. A wow affirms our beliefs and takes our breath away. Purpose tells us *why* we exist, and that directs every single *who*, *where*, *when*, *what*, and *how*.

Strategy created by *why* creates wows. So, let's begin with this first question in mind:

Why is your business here? If you can answer this question, your strategy will be clear. When we build brands by authentically asking *why*, we operate from a place of personal passion, deep-seated belief, intuitive knowing, empathic humanity, and creative liberation.

Wow turns consumers of goods into *presumers of good*—people who presume you are doing something meaningful. "Purpose takes us back to our origin, energizing our team members with our higher calling of connecting people, places, promises, and possibilities," says Laurie Tucker, senior vice president of corporate marketing at FedEx. "Our planes, trucks, hubs, and stores are the conduits we use to fulfill our purpose at FedEx. Every FedEx team member knows 'what' to do, but the passion for making every FedEx experience outstanding comes from our 'why.'"

Strategy is a direction. But the question becomes, who should set it? Should the marketplace or your distinctive place—your organization—determine strategy? If strategy is considered long term, how can it be part of a society that focuses on the short term?

The Three Ws of Strategy

When writing a purpose-driven strategy, it's helpful to remember the three Ws:

1. Who am I selling to? (your market)
2. What am I selling? (your product or service)
3. Why am I selling? (your reason for doing so)

In the past it was enough to know only who and what you were offering. When I was a copywriter in New York circa 1980, I worked on all sorts of products that had "two-W" strategies. The *who* for a toilet tissue brand might be female shoppers aged 24 to 39. The *what* might be softer and more absorbent. Initially, that was it. You shot clever commercials and hoped for the best.

If it didn't work, the agency would likely be fired and the new shop would change the strategy. This is no way to market with meaning. Adding the third W—the *why*—opens up an arena of possibilities. That toilet tissue might focus itself on a greater role in the world: providing sanitary conditions for the entire globe.

Strategy on purpose is not driven by the marketplace but by your distinctive place—your organization's role in the world. Much of strategy, however, is devised to fulfill shareholder expectations. But where does this leave the stakeholders, associates, partners, society, and the planet? We went to the top strategy firm to find out how they approach their own strategy through their own sense of purpose and culture.

BCG: The Birthplace of Strategy

The best place to learn about strategy is the place where the term *business strategy* was first used: the Boston Consulting Group (BCG).

Named to *Fortune* magazine's 100 Best Companies to Work For list seven years running and ranking in the top two for 2011 and 2012, BCG helps the world's leading firms develop and implement winning strategies. BCG's top strategist is senior partner and managing director Mike Deimler, who runs the firm's global strategy practice.

He sat down with me to talk about culture and how it drives strategy.

Deimler looks like a bit like Peter Parker, the man behind Spider-Man's mask. And he can spin a story as well as Spider-Man spins a web. According to Deimler, BCG's founder, Bruce Henderson, aspired to change the world the day he set up shop in 1963. So much so, he opened his second office in Tokyo shortly thereafter with the thought, "If you were going to change the world, you had better cover it." Later BCG was the first consulting firm in the world to be granted a license by the Chinese government to operate in China. Today, BCG has more than 75 offices in over 40 countries.

Henderson, the father of strategy consulting, was an iconic figure with, according to Deimler, a mantra to match. Quoting a line from the Greek mathematician Archimedes, "Give me a lever and a place to stand and I will change the world," Henderson would go on to remind his colleagues, "BCG is our place to stand, and our ideas are our levers. That's how we change the world."

One gets a true sense of greater purpose as Deimler channels his founder. "Bruce's strategy was to change the world by changing companies and entire industries. He would make change happen by shifting a client's perspective, and he would do that by the interchange of ideas among the world's finest thinkers."

Henderson mandated breakthrough insights. He was constantly bringing people together in a room and having massive skull sessions. "He would throw together a radically diverse set of really smart people, particularly for the time. Seasoned business veterans, recent college graduates, MBAs, and PhDs all at the same table, judged only on the quality of their contributions. Bruce brought in Sandy Moose, an economics PhD, in 1968—one of the first women in consulting and eventually BCG's first female partner."

"BCG will always invest ahead of the curve," Deimler added. For Deimler, this means focusing on culture and values as an integral aspect of building the firm. Today, BCG spends more than 100 hours getting to know each successful applicant. Walk through any of the firm's offices, and you will see a values statement prominently displayed. Come to a town hall meeting in the Atlanta office, and you will see the BCG values painted—2½ feet tall—around the perimeter of the room: Integrity, Respect for the Individual, Diversity, Clients Come First, The Strategic Perspective, Value Delivered, Partnership, Expanding the Art of the Possible, and Social Impact.

Collaboration, insight generation, and impact are at the heart of BCG's value proposition, but this sense of purpose has created a centrality of mission for all the partners and a collective commitment to use strategy as a lever to lift the world. This is a culture whose ethos is Henderson's eternal echo.

"Henderson's best strategy of all may have been, when he retired, giving his share of the firm he founded to his fellow partners for no consideration beyond their promise to do good," says Deimler. "If you're a partner at BCG, you have equity in the firm. It's the only major consulting partnership with a one-tiered system. Every partner gets a vote, and the best ideas win. Ideas are assessed by their impact on clients and on the world."

Were Henderson alive today, he would be celebrating BCG's 50th anniversary this year and would see his legacy of meaning at work in the firm's continued focus on social impact: in 2011 alone, BCG took on 200 pro bono projects for 120 different organizations, each trying to make the world a better place.

The Hero's Journey

American scholar Joseph Campbell discovered a pattern of narrative found in all great stories, a journey he has seen play out over and over again. He called it the Hero's Journey, an adventure story in which the hero achieves greatness on behalf of civilization or, in the case of *The Story of Purpose*, an organization.

Odysseus in *The Odyssey*, Jack and Rose in *Titanic*, and Dorothy in *The Wizard of Oz* are all heroes in this sense—people who were living predictable lives when they suddenly received a call to adventure. They were reluctant at first but took on the challenge, ridded the world of evil, and came home with some greater good for society.

So how does this affect your thinking as you lead your business, work to achieve a goal, and along the way, make a difference on your bottom line and humanity's purpose? It's simple. Let's look at the hero's strategy and an example that will illustrate my point.

Newell Rubbermaid Makes Purpose a Star

The 100-day journey would take us to three continents to gather insights from more than 300 leaders and associates. BrightHouse's most distinguished luminaries would further expand the team's perspective as to what role Newell Rubbermaid could play in the world. It turned out to be a starring one.

From Brands Bought to Brands That Matter

When Dan Ferguson was named president of Newell Companies in 1965, he saw an opportunity beyond curtain rods. Through a series of acquisitions, he grew the company from a small, one-category private company to a powerful hardware and housewares company. But its most significant acquisition was made in 1999 with the purchase of Rubbermaid, doubling the size of the company and creating Newell Rubbermaid.

By the time Mark Ketchum was named chief executive officer (CEO) in 2005, his company had gobbled up 70 brands in 30 years. The challenge now was to make the Newell name stand for something bigger than a federation of independent businesses. Greater purpose was needed. The words "Brands That Matter" were added to the company logo to emphasize his strategy.

The Parent Learns from the Child

I am often asked if purpose starts at the corporate level or in the brand. The answer is both. Each entity has its own DNA. Whereas P&G started at corporate, Newell Rubbermaid began at the brand level.

The beauty of starting at the top is that it sent a clear message to all brands that purpose is coming. Conversely, a great reason to start at the brand level is that you can use it as a test case. In Newell Rubbermaid's case, it started with Graco president Jay Gould's insistence that the children's products brand have greater meaning.

When Graco's purpose—"cradle those who cradle them"—was first introduced, employees were literally in tears, thanking me for recognizing their brand's true values. Purpose had reconnected Graco to its past, inspiring a purpose-driven strategy: to be more than just a stroller or car seat company but a parenting resource. Revenues grew almost 50 percent.

This purpose work had a domino effect that would enlist almost every Newell Rubbermaid brand to seek and tell the story of its purpose. "We had built a real fire inside the organization. And it spread," says Gould. Soon nearly all brands had discovered, articulated, and activated their purposes. Ketchum recognized the potential of some greater purpose to align Newell Rubbermaid's individual brands with that of the total corporation.

Illuminating What Matters

After completing the purpose work for 11 of Newell Rubbermaid's brands, BrightHouse then began the work on the corporate purpose and assembled a team of luminaries that included a historian, an evolutionary biologist, a neuroscientist, and philosopher Dr. Sam Keen. Two themes emerged in our synthesis: *successful systems are interdependent* and *what matters to people are authentic and meaningful stories that they can feel a part of*.

The team noted that healthy systems flourish when interdependent. Furthermore, brands that help people feel better about themselves create confident people who have the courage to live life fully. Now it was time to put it all together.

"Purpose is the glue between the brands and the company. We market everything from saw blades to strollers, but purpose brings us all together," says Ketchum.

Following are those values that make Newell Rubbermaid a standout when it comes to purpose companies.

Our Entrepreneurial Spirit Ignites Growth
Our Interdependence Drives Success
We Thrive through Innovation

Our Brands Inspire Passion
We Bring What Matters to Our Work

Looking for Values in All the Right Places

The journey had the team reconnect with key stories and attributes of the brands in order to coalesce the best qualities and turn them into values.

- **Our Entrepreneurial Spirit Ignites Growth:** United by a spirit that defined the company's beginnings, we would build upon the energy of our founders like Calphalon's Ron Kasperzak, Paper Mate's Patrick Frawley, and Vise Grip's Bill Petersen, clever individuals who defined an innovate or evaporate mind-set.

- **Our Interdependence Drives Success:** Saw blades can learn from strollers and pens from mops. Why not buy from one place rather than a dozen? Businesses under one roof work better together. Although each has a distinctive offering, they have one thing in common— all will be brands that matter to our stakeholders.

- **We Thrive through Innovation:** Our brands matter because they give people something to love, not just a premium price or margin. Tales of innovation from Rubbermaid, Paper Mate, Calphalon, Irwin Vise-grip, and Lenox tell a story of rapid innovation.

- **Our Brands Inspire Passion:** Graco's baby blog, Calphalon's Unison line, and Paper Mate's InkJoy line led a revolution in bringing out the best in people— and not just those in the marketplace but the proud associates at headquarters.

- **We Bring What Matters to Our Work:** Our people throw their whole selves—their expertise as businesspeople and their experience as human beings—into their work. It's not about work-life balance but work-life integration.

A Trick That I Wouldn't Trade

My mother Phylliss taught me a writing trick when I was in sixth grade that I have used ever since. After I had written an essay for school, she would have me read it to her. The last line was always the best. She said that was where the magic gets stored. So how can that help us discover your Master Idea?

Write a narrative using your values, and the last line of your story will contain a glimpse or maybe even your Master Idea. Take Newell Rubbermaid for example:

When Graco cradles caregivers so that they can cradle their babies, when Goody instills confidence through beauty and style and Irwin gives tradespeople the guts to grab the glory, when Calphalon brings people together by sharing their appetite for life, when Decor helps people create spaces to make themselves whole, when Lenox uses its passion to build it bigger and better, when Rubbermaid helps put life in order so that you can live it more fully, and when Paper Mate puts heart into connecting people with their imaginations, Newell Rubbermaid can claim its master idea and role in the world: "to help people flourish where they live, learn, work, and play." "I love the idea of flourish because it's the common thread for our leadership, employees, and a guiding light for a very complex portfolio," says Kristie Juster, 17-year veteran at Newell Rubbermaid and president of Graco. "It's what drives our strategy." (See Figure 7.1.)

FIGURE 7.1   Newell Rubbermaid Star
Source: Newell Rubbermaid.

Redefining the Plan to Win

Almost 7 billion people inhabit this planet. Of those, 800 million take part in the everyday workings of the global economy. Another 2.5 billion in emerging markets are readying themselves to join *the lucrative economy*. That still leaves more than 4 billion poor people who, given the chance to participate, could create new riches for all.

This win-win scenario redefines the plan to win. In this story, business grows because it helps people grow. Narrow strategy has reached its expiration date. This fresh approach encompasses the broadest market available—the world.

Economist Milton Friedman informed an entire generation of businesspeople that their primary strategy was to maximize profits. However, this strategy minimizes society by leaving more than half the world to fend for itself. The real growth market for business, then, is the people who *finally* are served. And the best strategy is one where all win.

Building a New Strategy to Cement the Future

Imagine that your strategy for growth focused on two-thirds of the world you had never thought about. Cemex, the largest cement company in the world, did just that. In 1994, after an economic downturn, Cemex was forced to look at its strategy. Leadership soon realized that all but the poorest people were pulling down sales. But hold on just a minute—those poor people were 40 percent of their business.

Company leadership issued a "declaration of ignorance," a message to itself that it had better get to know these people better. Managers were sent to shantytowns to see Cemex's most loyal constituency up close and in person. They learned that it took these no-choice-but-to-do-it-yourselfers 13 years to build a home due to their lack of money.

Cemex issued a program called *Patrimonio Hoy*—or equity—that allowed low-income families to obtain access to affordable solutions for building homes. For instance, 80 percent of all loans were financed without any prerequisites. Since the program first began operating in 2000, *Patrimonio Hoy* has provided affordable solutions to more than one million people throughout Latin America and has enabled more than 350,000 families to build their own homes.[2]

Cemex had found the mortar for success. By reducing poverty, the company had found the riches—spiritual and financial—of mitigating an ill in the world. This was a whole new strategy of incorporating the world's needs into the corporation's strategy. In *Capitalism at the Crossroads*, author Stuart L. Hart points out, "Margins are likely to be low (by current norms), but unit sales are extremely high." In this case, low margins spoke volumes.[3]

The bottom line for Hart—and for me—is that business must create strategy that sustains *life*, not just the business itself. Friedman's economics missed the economy of humanity, whose stock ebbs and flows with the confidence that we have in it.

Life's ethos has always been meaning; our cultures have always yearned for it. Our values guide us to it. Now our strategies must win back our rights to productive, happy, and healthy lives.

Competitive versus Distinctive Advantage

We also want to scrutinize the concept of *competition*. It's simply not sustainable to annihilate the other in an interdependent world. The word *competition* itself gives us a clue to a better strategy, as it comes from the Latin word *competere*, which means to "strive together."[4]

So where does that put the notion of competitive advantage? Business guru Michael Porter vetted the theory in 1985. A company or brand had competitive advantage if it had cost advantage or differentiation. But can this be the case in the modern world?

Given the speed that companies operate today and the massive geography they cover, brands' and organizations' advantages can be matched or subsumed instantaneously. Today's competitive advantage is tomorrow's parody or buyout. Furthermore, competitive advantage does not fit in the new lexicon of purpose. It is ephemeral and relies on strengths and weaknesses.

Years ago, I was invited to give a keynote at the Atlanta Competitive Advantage Conference (ACAC) titled Distinctive Advantage. I asked the audience the same question I ask you now: "What makes your company or brand distinct? What do you have that no other brand or organization possesses?" If you have what they have, you are dispensable. What you want is *indispensability*.

And only distinctiveness creates indispensability. Ask yourself, "What would the world be missing without *my* product or service?" If the answer is, "Nothing," then you have missed out on one of the many gifts of a purpose brand or company.

After all, even something disposable can be indispensable.

How to Be Indispensable

Dixie cups are the famous brand in their category and are disposables that are indispensable. To understand why, we journey back to their original purpose and the company strategy.

The story goes that two Boston men, Hugh Moore and Lawrence Luellen, were horrified by the 1907 use of dippers that allowed all people, including infectious ones, to dip ladles into public water cans. They called their invention the Health Kup, and their company was later renamed the Dixie Cup Company.

The Dixie business pored over its history to discover an ethos that was meaningful inside the organization: transforming behavior to improve life. The company was founded nearly a century ago on the belief that a simple change in behavior could lead to a monumental improvement in people's lives. With original purpose intact, how could we make this sentiment as true now for plates as it was then for cups? The strategy was this: provide the best disposable products that protect and foster what is indispensable—health, family, and time together. Minimize the meaningless—doing dishes—and maximize the meaningful or what was (and is) truly distinctive about your brand. The Dixie brand settled on its Master Idea "Be indispensable." This Master Idea was used internally by teams to help drive creativity around how they should think about the brand's role in consumers' lives. It provided the framework for thinking of new products and how the business talked to customers.

Today Dixie plates are the leading brand of disposable convenience plates in America, and Dixie products include a range of disposable cups, napkins, and plates that "Add convenience to today's families and help them make the most of their time."

Locate Your Black Box

Your purpose is timeless. Strategy, however, adapts to the times. When driven by your ethos, culture, and values, this black box strategy becomes the plan of action for your deep-seated mission. Graco's marketing strategy was driven by their purpose: "Cradle those who cradle them." They quickly moved the traditional marketing focus from traditional means to social and community marketing. The Graco blog has been an incredibly successful tool, providing a two-way conversation to help Mom in her parenting journey. Calphalon took its purpose—"Shared Is the Appetite for Life"—to heart by changing its marketing focus from product benefits to emotional benefits, thereby helping people come together to share the preparation and enjoyment of food. As Calphalon then–executive vice president and general manager, Kristie Juster, puts it, "There was always magic at Calphalon, but we struggled on how to describe that magic. Our purpose, 'Shared Is the Appetite for Life,' articulated that magic for the first time. Sharing is now our common charge. We used to have a laser focus on our product benefits, but with purpose it's all about how our consumers benefit."

Volvo cars have been known for their safety ever since the founders built automobiles that could handle Sweden's winding roads. That purpose drove Swedish inventor and Volvo employee Nils Bohlin to develop the first modern three-point seat belt used in most cars today. "In the United States alone, according to the National Highway Traffic Safety Administration, seat belts save more than 11,000 lives each year."[5]

Nutrition, health, and wellness company Nestlé's name means "little nest." As such, the company's ethos is in nurturing life. Their logo of a mother bird feeding her two baby birds illustrates the brand's moral and genuine purpose. By bringing the spirit of the nest to life internally and externally, Nestlé can nourish the bodies and souls of its employees as well as all the people who they feed today. With great purpose behind you, a strategy for a nobler world is ahead.

According to Nestlé marketing chief Tom Buday, "Nestlé's purpose is to enhance the quality of life with good food and beverages everywhere. This was true when our founder, Henri Nestlé, created an alternative source of infant nutrition for mothers unable to breast-feed, to combat infant mortality due to malnutrition. And, this remains true today, nearly 150 years later."

A strategy on purpose is single-mindedly focused. Its attraction is that it prevents distraction. Purposeful strategy gives organizations guardrails, not guidelines. Corporate heroes make their purpose personal, not just prescriptive. In the most dynamic and complex world in which we have ever lived, purpose-driven strategy provides associates with both a dream and the plan to get there. Whether it's a consultancy or cement company, purpose will help you build a strategy with a taller order.

What Is the Purpose of This Chapter?

- Purpose gives you *direction*. Strategy gives you the *directions*.
- Strategies are timely. Purpose is timeless.
- Purpose-driven strategy provides associates with both a dream and the plan to get there.

Purpose Pointers

- Work on *why* to get a wow.
- Be distinctive rather than competitive.
- Strategy is driven not by the marketplace, but by your place.

8

Tactics

All You Need Is Love

Why settle for loyalty when you can have love.

—Joey Reiman,
on stakeholder relationships

The Gulf Stream hits its temperature peak every July, meaning the water temperature is 86 degrees. One degree less, and you start shivering—and nothing gets you back once that happens. What 62-year-old world-famous swimmer Diana Nyad wanted for her 103-mile swim from Havana, Cuba, to Key West, Florida, is what sailors call the doldrums: a three-day window when the sea looks like glass. During the doldrums, your only problems are woman-eating sharks and poisonous box jellyfish.

Her secret is fearlessness—and her deodorant is Secret. And this is how marketing will be done in the future. Nyad's partnership is the result of purpose-powered branding from Procter & Gamble (P&G).

Love Is the Secret

Do you love your purpose? The answer to this question makes the difference between good marketing and great. When you fell in love with your soul mate, what did you tell him or her? "I love you." Then what did you do? You told everyone else! The best marketing works the same way. And with digital being the new media vehicle we love, there is no predicting how fast a meaningful message will travel—unless you know the secret.

Secret is one of P&G's billion-dollar brands—and purpose is a new brand-building initiative at P&G. Secret rolls out with a new purpose: "helping women of all ages become more fearless." Until recently, P&G marketers—like most—banked on their brand's point of difference. In Secret's case, this would be helping women become less fearful about sweating. Now with an inspiring point of view—"helping women of all ages become more fearless"—women fall in love with it. And they shout to the world.

In 1956, Secret became the first antiperspirant and deodorant made and marketed to women. The thinking behind it was that men and women have different needs when it comes to protection. But it was also a time when women entered the workforce in droves. This is what gives Secret greater purpose. Not only did it work best, but it now was a symbol of women going to work—something that was an act of fearlessness at that time.

Having sat on the board of the World TEAM Sports with Diana Nyad, I knew we had a winning formula on our hands: a powerful purpose from Secret and a human symbol that embodied it. Diana agreed, and so began the purpose-inspired partnership between Secret and Diana Nyad.

In the summer of 2010, inclement weather prevented Nyad from making her dream come true. However, she still managed to capture the dreams of thousands of women via

Facebook. The next summer, she took herself out of the water 59 miles from Havana due to poisonous jellyfish bites that shut down her lungs.

Although Nyad would have to put her dream on hold, she launched thousands of others. Her oceanic attempt to do what no human being has ever done before had a ripple effect with women around the world.

Word of Mouse Marketing

The effectiveness of purpose-driven tactics is a story told by the numbers. Linking Secret to Diana Nyad increased sales by double digits for Clinical Strength Waterproof, despite the fact that the product had been on the market for two years at that point.

The evolution of word-of-mouth marketing is word-of-mouse marketing. Secret's Facebook page became the second fastest growing page on the planet. Daily visitors increased by nearly 2,500 percent. Secret's latest purpose-inspired effort is "Mean Stinks," an antibullying campaign created by MEplusYOU. The company's Facebook page drew more than 200,000 fans in one day, with Secret experiencing significant double-digit growth in sales. Secret had not just built a better brand; it had created something that will replace *the brand* in the future. Secret had built a community. Brands are built with money. Communities are built with meaning.

Secret's Facebook fans numbered more than 1.5 million in 2012, when after 50 miles in, stings from lethal box jellyfish, inclement squalls, and thunderous lightning forced Nyad to abandon her fourth swim but sealed her legacy as one of the most purpose-driven women, forever.

The Secret brand team won accolades from P&G corporate, illustrating the power of purpose and how it could

move people from loyalty to love. There is no greater purpose in the world than love. And now *you* can use this secret
to activate purpose in your brand and company.

The Business of Love

Although love and business may seem like strange bed-
fellows, neuroscience tells us that at the heart of every
decision is a *heart* making the choice. The brain may run
everything else, but the heart runs the brain. And that's
why the heart is a significant chapter in this book on the
story of purpose.

I begin the ideation class I teach every semester with
this piece of advice: "Never marry anyone who is not a
friend of your excitement." Great personal relationships
happen between two people when you are each other's
cheerleaders. After 23 years of marriage, fanfare for the one
you love and what he or she loves is paramount. And brands
work the same way that people do. Whole Foods Market's
associates go out of their way to show customers they are
fans of their excitement by engaging in conversation. As an
example, a customer who purchased a turkey at a national
grocery chain burnt it on Thanksgiving Day. She called the
store to see if there were any turkeys left. Within hours,
another turkey arrived at her door with a chef who prepared it for her and her family. Whole Foods Market has
garnered something stronger than loyalty. Customers *love*
Whole Foods Market.

To better understand how love works and how we can
apply it to business, we turn to Dr. Robert Sternberg, pro-
vost and regents professor of psychology and education at
Oklahoma State University, who has spent the past 30 years
building a framework for love. According to Sternberg, love

is made up of three components: intimacy, passion, and commitment.

Passion + Intimacy = Romantic love
Intimacy + Commitment = Companion love
Passion + Commitment = Fatuous love
Passion + Intimacy + Commitment = Consummate Love

Passion involves physical attraction, intimacy involves sharing secrets, and commitment involves the decision to be in the relationship. He calls this the Triangle of Love. I call it the new marketing—emotionally charged messages that create super-charged messengers.

Having all three equals *consummate love* or as we call it, *brand union* (Figure 8.1). And here is the lesson: if you want to move from mere engagement to lasting meaningful relationships, you need to move people. If we draw correlates

FIGURE 8.1 BrightHouse Brand Union

Source: © BrightHouse. Illustration by David Paprocki.

for business from Sternberg's framework, we land on one that you can start using tomorrow.

Brand passion + Brand intimacy + Brand commitment = Brand union

Let's look at how this works through the lens of Secret's campaign with Diana Nyad.

Brand Passion

With every stroke Nyad takes, she exudes the passion of the brand. Secret successfully moved its product from under women's arms to inside their hearts. The dialogue created three summers ago is still going on right now—and Secret never let up. They have constancy of purpose evidenced by their passionate platforms, such as diving in with Diana and taking a strong stand on bullying.

Passion happens when issues move us. You have to uncover that issue in your own story of purpose. One way to do this: revisit the "Story Template" cartoon in the introduction and find your "once upon a time," your "suddenly," your "luckily," and your "happily ever after."

Brand Intimacy

In marketing, intimacy is created through sharing, which we do by using purpose as a vehicle to tell a story, as well as to listen to people's responses. The Latin root of the word *communication* is *communicatio*, which also means "to share."[1] Having an ongoing dialogue, not a traditional media monologue, is the genius of platforms such as Facebook and Twitter. **How does your company share stories with associates and customers?**

Brand Commitment

Commitments aren't made on spreadsheets or media schedules. They are made on the day the brand or company is born, and they must be demonstrated every day thereafter. Starbucks demonstrates its commitment to higher-order ideals 24/7. On Independence Day of 2012, Starbucks chairman, president, and chief executive officer (CEO) Howard Schultz asked our nation's leaders to put partisanship aside in search of partnerships for real solutions. To spark the conversation, Starbucks invited America on July 4 to come into Starbucks for a free cup of coffee.[2]

Love Is a Super Market

Although an unlikely candidate as a model for business, a boutique summer resort food market in New York State's Fire Island fits the bill.

Seaview Market stands as a model for the prosperity that comes to a company that loves having you as a customer. Rather than focusing solely on operational excellence and efficiencies, they have built their success on practicing the art of loving.

Passion for your product is the best practice. Passion guarantees constant improvement—in the Seaview Market case, fresher and fresher ingredients sourced from the best resources ensure surprise and delight.

Communicating with your customers and responding to them creates intimacy. In the Seaview Market case, the owner found out that our youngest son, Julien, liked Cocoa Puffs, a product found only on the mainland. The next morning we found it on our kitchen table.

And finally, commitment. Passion and intimacy without commitment is at best a one-night stand or a one-day customer. Commitment takes daily acts of love and caring, just as any healthy relationship does.

During our family's latest sojourn to Fire Island, the owners not only sourced swordfish hooked the night before but prepared it to perfection and served it dockside. The spread included our two favorite bottles of wine. We were so moved by their gesture we gave them credit for the vintage sunset as well.

By loving their customers in the most genuine of ways, this little market teaches business the biggest lesson of all.

Love Begins at Home

In this case, home would mean the office. Purpose-powered companies take care of associates so that associates can take care of their customers. By living the passion, sharing intimately, and committing to the promise internally, people learn how to execute it externally.

Company Passion

Nike's headquarters translates the passion of its brand through state-of-the-art fitness studios, an Olympic-sized pool, two soccer fields, a basketball court, a 400-meter track, and a putting green.[3] In November 2010, Google put its passion into employees' pockets with a $1,000 cash bonus and 10 percent raise.[4]

Since opening the doors of BrightHouse, thinkers inside the company receive a Gift of Life bonus. That is, when an associate has a baby, his or her loved one receives a $500 bonus and a welcome to the BrightHouse family.

The Whole Foods Market headquarters in Austin, Texas, has a large rooftop plaza with an area that's used for live music during the summer and converted into a public skating rink in the winter.

As people spend more time at the office at Newell Rubbermaid headquarters, the company saves time for its staff with a full-purpose gym and dry cleaning services on campus.

And one of the guiding principles as to why Nordstrom is successful comes from *The Nordstrom Way:* "Nordstrom empowers its employees with the freedom to make decisions, and is willing to live with those decisions. Delegating authority and accountability is the ultimate expression of leadership."[5]

Company Sharing

3M, a manufacturing company that creates tens of thousands of products, including adhesives, laminates, and abrasives, believes in sharing knowledge across teams to create the best ideas and innovations. The company has regular knowledge-sharing meetings and has even created the Technical Council for the heads of the various labs to meet regularly and share ideas.[6] Walmart offers a voluntary Personal Sustainability Program that works with interested employees to create programs that have a positive impact on the environment, their communities, and their health.[7]

Company Commitment

Most people have heard tales of the great perks one receives when working at Google: laundry rooms, organic food, gyms, massages, bike repair, and on-site doctors and barbers— all given to employees to let them know they are appreciated. Southwest Airlines has a no-layoff policy.[8] Even during the aftermath of 9/11, where their competitors were laying off their workforces, Southwest held strong to this belief to protect the company's long-term health and employee loyalty and love. And motorcycle maker Harley Davidson created the Learning Center, a venue that's dedicated to providing resources for employees to experience lifelong learning.[9]

There has been much said and written about *relationship marketing*. But there's an important distinction to make here: not all relationships are created equally. As we have learned from Sternberg, there are at least three kinds of relationship marketing. The best of these is consummate love, or what we call brand union. Like a good marriage, brand union unifies two to create a third entity: a relationship for life. Here, what you buy is what you buy into. As Emory professor Dr. Rick Gilkey states, "It's the difference between that's mine and that's me." Apple fanatics are an example of people who at their own core imbue the character or ethos of the brand.

What Brand Do You Love?

To make an important point about love, I ask my class every semester this question: "What brand do you love?" Almost all of them have the same answer: "Apple." Then, I ask if any of their Apples are lemons; that is, did they ever break? All hands go up. So Apple products aren't perfect. I ask, "Do you still love Apple?" "Yes," they say. My next question is then, "What brand do you hate?" The unanimous response comes back: "the cable company."

The lesson here is that nothing is more powerful than love, for people or for products. Apple is passionate about the letter "i". iPods, iPads, and I the person. Apple makes you feel special. Apps are the way you share that passion with the world. And commitment? Just when you think you have the coolest device, Apple comes out with a cooler one. Ask yourself: "What brands do you love? What logos make you smile?" And what is it about both of these that cause such a positive reaction? As Professor Jag Sheth wrote in his purpose-filled book *Firms of Endearment*, "endearing companies tend to be enduring companies."[10]

You Scratch My Brand, I'll Scratch Yours

Legendary marriages and marketing have another defining characteristic. They begin with *a mint on your pillow*. When you get something nice, you want to give back.

A fledgling new company called Hiya Media, known simply as hiya!, has taken product trial into the twenty-first century by using social media to allow people to send product samples to one another as gifts. Independent director Paul Woolmington calls it social sampling. The advent of purpose will cause businesses to work a whole new, and more loving, way. Chief marketing officers will act more like chief marriage officers who counsel their companies and brands on how to create authentic genuine relationships at headquarters and with customers in every corner of the world. Benevolent actions on the part of companies will replace advertising blitzes from agencies. Say goodbye to old words such as *consumers, targets, segmentation, reach and frequency, impressions, points of difference, integrated marketing*, (not so) *unique selling propositions, media buys* (won't have to), and even the concept of brand as we know it.

Darwin Pays a Visit to Marketing

The word *brand* comes from the Old English word *brand* or *brond*, meaning "fire, flame; firebrand, piece of burning wood, torch."[11] Nineteenth-century blacksmiths (not marketing mavens) created branding. Without any way to earmark and catalog livestock, branding irons seared logos onto the hides and rumps of cattle, sending a clear signal— "I own it"—from one rancher to another.

In one fell swoop, branding became red hot as a statement of ownership. And not much has changed over the course of a century. Business has branded just about everything in what will be known as the largest human experiment in civilization's history: advertising.

It didn't take long for the world to become ad rich and idea poor. That's when I saw the possibility for business, marketers, and ad agencies to become agents of change for the better. I saw BrightHouse as something that could serve as the laboratory for this new experiment. When I think of the future of business, I am reminded of Charles Darwin, whose science of evolution has finally found its way to business. Some observations about the evolution of our marketing world:

- **Brand versus stand:** A rose is one of tens of thousands of species of flowers. Fragrant and beautiful, it stands for something more: love. Thanks to author William Shakespeare and marketer Hallmark, the rose has been imbued with the ineffable. A brand is a promise. A stand is the promise of something greater. What does your brand stand for?
- **Communication brief versus community brief:** Today, marketers use communication briefs as blueprints for building campaigns. Tomorrow, they will build communities. As a brand architect, Secret built a community of more than a million women online. They now own the brand because it is their community. Marketers used to be aggregators of customers, but facilitating their connections appears to be a much better bet.
- **Media buy versus free media:** If you're still spending money on media, you have the wrong message.

Purpose + Social Media = Big Savings and Impact. Carlsberg beer created a viral film titled "Bikers" based on its purpose: "Courage brews in each of us." The video accumulated more than 11.4 million hits.

- **Employees versus volunteers:** About 23 million millennials who care more about purpose than profit wear pajamas instead of suits and work in the age of "no age is too young." Millennials don't sign up for jobs; they enlist in causes and movements. And according to the Cone Study on millennials, nearly 89 percent of them want brands with great meaning. This presents an enormous opportunity for purpose companies who want to attract a generation who puts meaning over money.[12]

- **Point of difference versus point of view:** Whom would you rather have dinner with: a point of difference or a point of view? Product benefits in and of themselves are no longer enough. People want to know your point of view, your purpose. "Don't be evil" is Google's point of view. Originally suggested by Paul Buchheit, a Google employee and the creator of Gmail, it delivers a strong message that in the long term, we will be better served as shareholders and in all other ways by a company that does good things for the world, even if we forgo some short-term gains.[13]

- **Loyalty versus love:** Passion for your customer, dialogue, and constancy of purpose—the pillars of love—are what create a union with your associates and customers. Boston Consulting Group's founder was passionate, creating a dialogue with the world—and the employees continue his work every day.

- **Ads versus actions:** Starbucks spends only 1 percent of system sales on marketing. For Starbucks, ads don't add as many customers as actions do.[14] The latest action came from the CEO, Howard Schultz, who took out a full-page ad on July 4 in the *New York Times* asking business and government to work together in making the United States work better. To start the conversation, he invited all of us in for a free cup of coffee. The bean growers and bean counters were very happy.

The Evolution of Business

The word *philanthropy* comes from the Greek, *phil*, meaning "loving," and *anthropos*, meaning "mankind."[15] Loving humankind is the work of philanthropy, which is now finding its way into mainstream business. Edie Fraser, CEO of STEMconnector.org and senior consultant of Diversified Search, stated, "It has been a joy to align business interests with making money and giving back. It started early in my life with five exchange programs, five years working for the Peace Corps, and five years as a consultant to the Nation's Poverty Program."

Edie continues, "Business, though, was in my blood. So I took on many social causes when I started my PR firm and then many policy issues. Then I seized on diversity with support of Women and People of Color as well as GLBT and other rights." Edie is just one example where purpose, although not philanthropy itself, helps drives philanthropy that is relevant and authentic to your company and thrives when your company is dedicated to the well-being of others.

It's clear that love is the central heartbeat of purpose and ideas that last, including the products, services, and concepts that make you feel whole. They begin and end with businesses that work their way into your heart. Love it or leave it. Now, let's go build your purpose.

What Is the Purpose of This Chapter?

- The brain runs everything, and the heart runs the brain.
- Purpose moves people from loyalty to love.
- There is no greater purpose in the world than love.

Purpose Pointers

- Purpose moves us from engagement to brand union.
- Put your heart into your brand.
- Put purpose at the heart of everything.

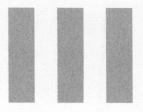

Purpose, Inc.

How to Incorporate Purpose into Your Business

Four I's see better than two.

—Joey Reiman,
on visioning

Chances are that as time has passed, your organization's original idea has become buried under a mountain of distractions: leadership changes, quarterly goals, mergers, and corporate initiatives. Suddenly, your company or brand is simply doing what it must to compete in the marketplace rather than building on its earliest distinctive ideals. Recounting our beginnings allows us to get back to the original story.

My framework for rediscovering your story is called the Four I's Ideation Process (Figure P.III.1).

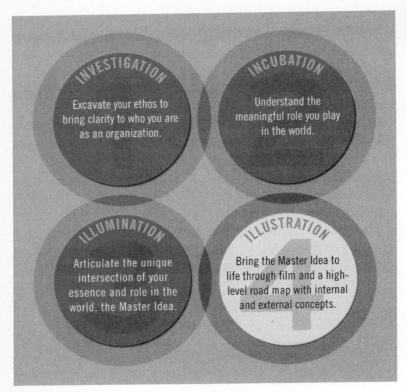

FIGURE P.III.1   The BrightHouse Four I's Process

Source: © BrightHouse. Illustration by David Paprocki.

This structured method of thinking has served hundreds of companies as a way to discover, articulate, activate, and incorporate purpose into your company or brand.

Inspired by physiologist and physicist Hermann von Helmholtz, who graduated from the Medical Institute in Berlin in 1843, this multistep process serves as the foundation for our process. It will take our thinking through the gathering of information and data—*investigation* to thoughtful *incubation*—and onward to the unprecedented insight that results in *illumination* and *illustration*. It has taken our brains 4 billion years of evolution to think this way, so why not use our heads correctly?

We begin our 16-week journey with an investigation to identify your organization's unique talents and values. Think dramatic television series *CSI*; only for our purposes, the acronym stands for corporate soul investigation. We are looking for the truth.

The next step is incubation; this is where you'll begin to think about your organization's role in the world, specifically, why your brand matters to society. Subject matter experts—luminaries—will now join the team to expand your thinking and contemplate connections and some unexpected combinations that will help your enterprise optimize people and profits. Borrowing a page from Albert Einstein, if investigation is knowledge, then incubation is imagination and "imagination is more important than knowledge."[1]

Illumination takes your team to the intersection of your company's unique gift and the world's needs. The work now is in position to illuminate all facets of your business.

Illustration is how you will illustrate your purpose internally and externally. How can we *be*, *do*, and *say* purpose? We must *be* authentic, *do* things that show we mean it, and *say* it the right way—all of which are in service of aligning your organization's ideals, strategies, and people with greater purpose for bigger outcomes and incomes.

Here's where your story kicks off. From this point forward until the end of Part III, your DBA (Doing Business As) is Purpose, Inc. Let's open the doors.

9

Investigation

Questions are the new answers.

—Joey Reiman,
on Investigation

F ictional detective Sherlock Holmes was famous for his extra-keen powers of observation, which he used to solve perplexing mysteries. *You* are Sherlock Holmes in the first step of the Four I's Ideation Process; in other words, you're the detective. Your job is to collect as much data as possible from your company or brand. That means going back to your beginnings and gathering "clues" from those who hold the cherished stories of your organization.

Investigation also requires that you observe your company's culture. You can do this by asking lots of questions of all your associates, from the top floor to the factory floor. Our typical process at BrightHouse is to interview 30 people in a company over 1-2 weeks to get a good idea of what the enterprise stands for and where it wants to go.

To find out what role your organization plays in the world, you need to discover what makes it unique and special. Once the detective work is done, we can start to hypothesize on themes that will eventually lead the team to a Master Idea and bring your company into its future.

Think about what it's like when you first start dating someone. You may have met online and read his or her profile, or you may have a friend who set you up. You know the basic information about your date: name, occupation, likes, and dislikes. But you want to know what this person is *really* like when you meet him or her, not the "best of me" version presented during those first few dates. Who is his or her authentic self?

BrightHouse goes through the same process with companies. We get beyond the "best of me" presentations found on websites and in public relations (PR) materials to discover a company's core. To get to an organization's real essence, BrightHouse takes an organization that wants to incorporate purpose into its system through an investigation process that has four discriminate parts:

- Review existing primary and secondary data.
- Conduct interviews with leaders and constituents.
- Excavate brand ethos and review historical materials and story.
- Prepare and deliver investigation synthesis.

Our process is similar to Sherlock Holmes's process, although there is no blood and very little pipe smoking involved. Our investigation digs deep, beyond the obvious.

First, Search the Research

Our first step is to thoroughly study all materials. First up are market, cultural, and competitive reports; then we think like Sherlock Holmes, magnifying glass in hand, and focus on what might seem inconsequential—a scrap of thread, the stub of a cigar, and so on. For us, like any good detective, these pieces of evidence are the clues we need.

And as far as we're concerned, the more, the better. For example, one client took our passion to heart and sent over two pallets of historical materials. It included everything from the company's first ads to catalogs from every year the company had been in business to company picnic pictures, to news clippings, to photos of the chief executive officer's family. We didn't find it overwhelming; we welcomed it with open arms.

Other signposts of a company's Master Idea include past speeches, newsletters, annual reports, operating frameworks, and always, stories, stories, stories, and more stories.

The More Questions You Ask, the More Answers You Get

As BrightHouse luminary and philosopher Dr. Sam Keen said, "Searching, longing, and questioning is in our DNA. Who we are and what we will become is determined by the questions that animate us, and by those we refuse to ask. As you ask, so shall you be."

WellPoint is the largest health care company in America. With the health care industry in a state of flux, the organization's leadership decided to excavate the company's purpose. Our strategists asked chief marketing officer Kate Quinn during the investigation phase, "What would the world lose without WellPoint?"

She proudly answered, "The heart of health care." This valuable input gave both BrightHouse and WellPoint a sense of its corporate self. How would you describe the corporate self of your organization? And what would the world lose if your company no longer existed? Ask yourself and your colleagues.

Ethos, company culture, visions, leadership, and stories of origins are all clues to solving the mystery of who your authentic corporate self is.

Marketing partners from consultancies to advertising agencies often encourage organizations to reflect marketplace desires. However, that approach only leads companies to do and make the same stuff. Worse, it keeps an organization from fulfilling its own true destiny. Trying to be something you're not doesn't work in a world that demands authenticity. But when your story comes from the founders' hearts, you could even make up where your product came from.

Take ice cream maker Häagen-Dazs, for example. It is the ice cream with the Danish sounding name and original labels that included an outline of Denmark. But many people would be surprised to know that the founders were two Polish immigrants from the Bronx. The ice cream was named Häagen-Dazs because the name rang of the old-world values of goodness—pure products—and because Denmark exhibited goodness to the Jews during World War II.[1] This story made *me* melt—and I have been eating their ice cream ever since.

In Search of Your Destiny

Our second step in investigation begins in the C-suite by conducting what we call destiny sessions. These gatherings are designed to give us a picture of an organization's future. We interview senior and mid-level managers, because these are the people who have the power to take the organization to the next level—to steer the ship and not just drift in the current. We need to hear their hopes, dreams, and highest aspirations.

What do you believe your organization could accomplish in 5, 10, 20, or 100 years if all obstacles were removed? What is your personal dream for your brand or company? What greater role do you believe it could play in the world? What's your favorite story?

Maggie Schear, a senior strategist for BrightHouse, has participated in many of these destiny sessions in which we interview one leader at a time. She explains the process: "We focus on each leader's vision, what they hope their legacy will be, and why they have chosen to take this role. We want to hear about the impact they hope to have on the world. We use their insights to unearth the ethotic themes."

We then expand the pool of interviewees to include company associates. Let's do an interview. Write your answers next to the following questions that we often use.

- Why did you join your organization?
- How would you describe the culture at your organization? How is it today compared with when you first joined? What is the same, and what is different?
- Which of your own personal values do you believe are also consistent with your organization's values?
- What do you believe is most unique or distinct about your organization?
- If you had a magic wand and there were no obstacles in your way, what is the *one* thing you would change about the organization? And what would you never change?
- If your organization was gone tomorrow, what would the world lose? ("Shareholder value" is not an acceptable answer.)

"We use these interviews to determine the organization's values, which we articulate in the unique language of the organization so that they are distinctive, ownable, and memorable," Schear said. "Once we identify key themes, we go back to the interviews for information that supports those themes." These constituent interviews are also invaluable for learning more about the brand's recent history. We always ask people to tell us their favorite stories about their organization. Those add to the knowledge we acquire about the company's history and unique personality. Now it's your turn. What is your favorite story?

When you ask a person what his or her favorite story is, you learn a lot. Sam Keen said, "Stories help people recognize not only what matters to them individually but that they belong to a group."

Another major benefit of these constituent interviews is that they involve your associates in arguably the most important effort your organization will ever mount—the search for soul. According to Schear, "By conducting these interviews, managers are telling employees that leadership is interested in their voices. Some companies we work with have had internal cultural challenges, pain points in the organization. The mere fact that we're conducting the interviews means a lot."

We want to know what these people value about their company, what engages their imagination, because these elements are critical to determining its future.

Digging for Ethos

The NBC television show *Who Do You Think You Are?* features celebrities who are tracing their family's trees to discover their roots—and often discovering surprising things in their past. Their ancestors may have been community leaders, or they may have been slave owners or murderers.

The second step in investigation—excavating the brand ethos—requires that companies undergo a similar process and ask, "Who do we think we are?" Just like people, every company has a story of origin. And the results of such a search can be equally enlightening. Identifying what made a company great in the first place provides the basis for thinking about its capacity to affect public life.

This isn't about reviving the past. It's about understanding what made the company thrive and why it is what it is today. It's an excavation to uncover the basic truths about the company, which will serve to illuminate the path ahead.

My class at Emory has been conducting these historical digs for years, and they've uncovered some amazing, powerful stuff. For example, did you know that one of Barnes & Noble's founders, Charles Barnes, was a visionary who began selling books from his home in Wheaton, Illinois?[2] He was so motivated to spread knowledge that he sold books out of a wheelbarrow.

Money Is the Root of All Good

SunTrust Bank's ethos of bringing financial well-being to the world has been a beacon throughout its history. From bringing investment back to the Civil War–ravaged South to being one of the few financial institutions to stay solvent during the Great Depression, SunTrust has built its enterprise—clients, teammates, shareholders, and communities—upon its foundation of noble work. What would people think of your company if you had a compelling background story like this one? They likely would be drawn in just as you were. This is an important part of uncovering your story of purpose.

Investigating the World

What if you are looking for a Master Idea for a global organization? Master Ideas cross borders, because they coalesce the shared beliefs of all countries involved, as we saw in the Carlsberg Group. Truth translates into every language.

Carlsberg was founded in 1847 by the visionary brewer J. C. Jacobsen, a leader in pioneering steam brewing and refrigeration techniques. J. C. and his son Carl developed a method to propagate a single strain of yeast, which revolutionized the brewing industry. That single experiment created the fourth largest brewery in the world, with hundreds of brands and more than 41,000 employees.

BrightHouse conducted more than 35 leadership interviews with people in all departments of Carlsberg all over the world, from Denmark to Russia to Asia. Themes began to emerge from those interviews, themes we could explore further with the constituent interviews. Associates and employees of all levels at the company, from marketing directors to strategy directors to a brewery manager and full circle to the director of the Carlsberg Museum, all participated in this process.

Constituent interviews with Carlsberg associates found that they were timid about saying "We're the best"; in fact, they felt a little bit like an underdog in the overcrowded realm of beer suppliers. They were looking to recapture Carlsberg's winning spirit—so in a courageous move, the Carlsberg Group ordered their company to "thirst for great." During the interviews, the one thing we found across nearly 500 brands is a passion for achieving greatness. Despite nationality, geography, or product, these brands burned to excel.

Courage to Do What You Love

Another courageous act took place in my hometown, Atlanta. At the intersection of women spending 85 cents of every dollar and being almost nonexistent in the highest places of business, my wife Cynthia Good had the courage to build a company dedicated to advancing women in the workplace, a company that now reaches more than 100,000 career women every morning.

LittlePinkBook.com is the number one online resource for working women and a testament to Cynthia's and the company's purpose: "Courage to do what you love."

"Our purpose redefined the meaning of success, which drives everything about Little Pink Book," says Cynthia. "It's clearly an idea that speaks directly to women's authenticity."

"When we started the investigation process, I figured we'd end up with values all relating to business as a way to define success." Instead the group found its driving values were beauty, freedom, courage, and the belief that having a beautiful career was the means to a beautiful life.

"When I speak to groups of women, I tell them, I don't care how important you are. If you don't love what you are doing and can't connect with your work, then it's not who you are," Cynthia said.

And as Dr. Keen puts its, "A society in which a calling and job are separated for most people gradually creates an economy that is often devoid of spirit, one that frequently fills our pocketbooks at the cost of emptying our souls."

Raising the Standard

Jay Gould, chief executive officer of American Standard, has been both around the block and around the world spreading the gospel of purpose. Gould asked me to meet him at the Mandarin hotel to hear an idea he had for American Standard. Anyone who has been in a bathroom knows the name and probably agrees that higher-order ideals don't come to mind when you say it.

"I want to raise the standard," Jay told me. "In my company and in the world." Immediately, my image of American Standard changed. (Didn't yours?)

When BrightHouse conducted interviews at American Standard, sure enough, we found that the support was there. Three themes rose to the top: health, performing beautifully, and responsibility. Here are excerpts about each from just a few interviews:

- **On health:** "What excites me most about American Standard is the dedication of the people and the notion that we have the capability of improving people's lives and health in a meaningful way."
- **On performing beautifully:** "Three words to describe American Standard: foolproof, reliable, beautiful." "The brand is about beauty and utility for your life, in your kitchen and bathroom."
- **On responsibility:** "We're doing a great job on conservation. [By using] us, you conserve water without sacrificing performance. We don't charge more for you to be comfortable or eco-friendly; we are inherently responsible."

From Toms to Johns

If the idea of giving a pair of shoes to those who can't afford them for every pair you buy appeals to you, what purpose leader Jay Gould is about to do will floor you. American Standard will partner with The Bill and Melinda Gates Foundation to improve safety and sanitation in developing countries.

In 2013, for every Champion toilet you purchase from American Standard, they will deliver a latrine to an under-served family in Bangladesh. Says Gould, "This could be the new American Standard for business."

The Sum Is Bigger Than Its Parts

After all interviews and research are complete, we pull our findings together into a synthesis, a combination of elements to make something new. From here we develop ethotic themes, the clues that lead us to an organization's true character. And just like in detective stories, the process of investigation is always the same. But the outcome never is.

Take the story of Paper Mate. Patrick J. Frawley's determination to find an ink that didn't clog, skip, or smear led the Frawley Pen Company to develop a fast-drying ink and the creation of the Paper Mate pen.

Ethotic themes that flowed from our work with Paper Mate included a *flair for innovation, indelible reliability, a write-on attitude, everywhere is the point,* and *you can't beat two hearts.* We then took these themes and explored them in our next step: incubation. Clients are often wildly surprised by the synthesis formed from the incubation process. This is where the true magic happens.

As we wrap up this chapter, it is clear that the process of uncovering a company's ethos will inevitably reveal the true "corporate self." Only from an authentic core can a company then look at the role it can play in the world—the next stop on its journey to create a Master Idea that will guide and inspire the organization and bring a positive presence to the world.

So consider these questions as you move forward: What are the distinctive and authentic strengths of *your* company or brand? What is your story of origin? What is your company dream? Is it the same as your own?

With some answers in hand—and what we call ethotic themes or high-interest areas—we can now move to incubation. In this process, mindful people called luminaries will help us create the company you have only imagined up until now.

What Is the Purpose of This Chapter?

- Ethos, company culture, visions, leadership, and stories of origins are clues to solving the mystery of who your authentic corporate self is.
- Investigation is about converging all inputs into a concise output—the shared beliefs from factory floor to top floor.
- It's not about analysis, it's about synthesis.

Purpose Pointers

- Investigation is about excavation, not creation.
- The right questions lead to the correct answers.
- If you want to reach high, dig deep.

10

Incubation

I think for a living.

—Joey Reiman,
on Incubation

Fast thinking is an oxymoron. In fact, we consider *fast* a four-letter word at BrightHouse. We know that the work of purpose demands thoughtfulness, especially during the incubation phase of the Four I's Ideation Process.

Ben Franklin credits good relations between France and America during revolutionary times to the fact that slow ships were carrying sensitive and important messages back and forth across the Atlantic Ocean.[1] This gave each side time to think—and led to the expression *floating the idea*.

Today, *we shoot the idea over* via chat, text, tweets, blogs, Skype, pins, and tags. We have traveled from frigate speed to warp speed to warped speed. And we are paying for it. Fasting through the day has us starving for thought-filled thinking. But crafting a purpose takes thought. And thought takes time.

Business at the Speed of Molasses

When thinking is not possible, it becomes impossible to come up with thoughtful solutions. This is why we established incubation sessions; these meetings create a time of necessary contemplation that companies need to imagine the role they can play in the world. Businesses usually don't work this way, which is precisely the reason that their plans don't always work out.

Here's an example that speaks to this concept: thousands of people are members of something called the Slow Food movement. The movement's underlying concept is recognizing that we can enhance the pleasure we take in consuming food when we have a better understanding of where it comes from. Food lovers, restaurant patrons, and farmers themselves come together with the purpose of enjoying one another and bringing meaning to meals. Sounds delicious, doesn't it?

Think of the process of incubation as a Slow *Think* movement for your company. It's a way to reconnect with its roots as it explores better ways to connect with the world. During this 16-week journey of purpose, you and your colleagues will spend 4 weeks moving from wondering what comes next to absolute wonder—the moment of illumination.

In classical Greece, incubation was a practice where a person performed a ritual act and then went to sleep in a sacred place, hoping to receive a divinely inspired dream (or cure, if the person was ill). In our case, the goal is to discover how your company can inspire the world—or find a cure for what ails it. We have learned after thousands of hours of incubation that time is revealing and essential in your story of purpose. As they say, *only time will tell*.

Heartstorming: The New Brainstorming

The word *brainstorm* was originally used in 1890 to mean chaos that resulted in disturbance. In 1953, Alex Osborn, the O in famed BBDO advertising agency, popularized the modern use of the word *brainstorming* to mean a group effort to come up with new solutions.

Since then, brainstorming has been the accepted method for fostering creativity in the business world. In fact, it's become so popular that most people assume that creativity and innovation have to be group processes.

This probably won't come as a surprise, but I don't believe in brainstorming. For me, this concept calls up the original meaning, which makes me think of depression and anxiety—a disturbance in the brain. Disrupting a thought is not the goal; quietly nurturing the idea is.

Recent research backs me up. Professor of psychology and education at Washington University and *Explaining Creativity* author Keith Sawyer states, "Decades of research have consistently shown that brainstorming groups think of far fewer ideas than the same number of people who work alone and later pool their ideas."[2]

The goal of an incubation session is not to come *up* with the idea, but to come *in* with the idea. All too often people show up to brainstorming sessions empty-headed. That's why I prefer *heartstorming*, sessions where thinkers have taken the problem they are trying to solve to heart. That means they have deeply studied their subject matter and come up with possible solutions before they walk into the room.

When participants arrive at an incubation session, they come with an open heart, that is, an openness to others' ideas. In this way, heartstorming gets to the heart of the real matter and prompts everyone involved to ask themselves, "How will my ideas make the world a brighter place?"

In heartstorming we:

- Take it to heart.
- Open our hearts.
- Get to the heart of the *real matter*.

Putting more heart into thinking creates better, bigger, and more meaningful ideas. And they don't come from just you but from people who have put their hearts into their work throughout their lives.

And Then There Was Light

Getting to the real heart of the matter requires more than a bunch of businesspeople in a room with giant Post-it boards. You need *luminaries*, subject matter experts who shed billion-watt light on what is keeping you in the dark.

These thought leaders have the perspective, knowledge, and wisdom to help teams figure out how to make their brand or company as large as the world in which they work. Luminaries are cherry-picked; they help us create a "Purpose, Inc." tank of hyperfocused, subject mastering experts from many different industries. They have cast a wide net over a topic and bring accelerated clarity.

More than 300 BrightHouse luminaries have spent their lives studying, writing, experimenting, and creating within their given fields. When they come to an incubation session, they bring deep insights right out of the gate. I hope that the hours and years I've spent with them will come through on the pages of this chapter and that I can use the experiences to give you something to think about—and a way to find your own story of purpose.

Our clients are smart enough to know businesses can't fix the problems in their organizations with the same people who created them. So how do you get started on solving the problems—and who do you invite to help you? Let's start by taking a close look at what you'll be doing and how you'll get it done.

The Modern-Day Algonquin Round Table

The Algonquin Round Table was the name given for a gathering of the country's greatest writers, actors, and humorists who ate lunch together on a regular basis from 1919 to 1929. They came together at the Algonquin Hotel in New York, the heartbeat of the literary world and a place where their creative collaborations gained national attention.[3]

I like to think of our incubation sessions as an Algonquin Round Table of sorts. They are scenarios where we gather the most brilliant people in the world to discuss your company, its purpose, and how it might change the world.

Luminaries fly into Hartsfield-Jackson Atlanta International Airport from all over the planet. They gather at BrightHouse, an 80-year-old two-story red brick building near downtown Atlanta that was originally a bank. Befittingly, the incubation room used to be the bank's vault, the place where the most valuable items were kept.

Because luminaries are subject matter experts, they bring divergent thinking to the subject you are working on. In this way, they expand our thinking and arena of possibility. For instance, if you are in the hotel industry, we don't need an expert on hospitality as much as an anthropologist who can talk about our human need to have someone waiting for us when we get home. That valuable insight will surely spark new ideas.

BrightHouse spends weeks selecting the right luminaries. We conduct a diligent and thorough exploration to find not only the right people, but the right combination of people, complementary to one another—just like you would for a good dinner party.

Luminary sessions are not focus groups. Rather, they are focused on the possibilities you see when you gaze through the lens of purpose. We are not testing copy; we are testing the courage of companies to make the world better and brighter. Luminaries don't come to the table with new-fangled ideas for your products and services. They arrive with fresh ways for your organization to think about its greater role in society. Luminaries don't help you sell; they help you *tell* your story of purpose.

The brick-and-glass-enclosed room is airy, with elements of light everywhere, from the white chandelier hanging from the 14-foot ceilings to the natural light streaming in. With a bookshelf filled with volumes written by our luminaries, BrightHouse strategists, luminaries, and our clients gather around a 12-foot-long table. We have no squeeze balls or other paraphernalia often used in brainstorming sessions.

Our rule is no more than 12 people; another is never after 12 PM. We don't want more than a dozen individuals present, and we always meet in the morning. Any food that's served is light fare. And although the environment is carefully orchestrated, our conversations never are.

After 17 years of conducting these sessions, there has never been one where something remarkable, meaningful, and surprising has *not* been revealed. I've spent the most important hours of my career in these sessions.

"It's rather unexpected for our clients at first," said Monika Nikore, BrightHouse senior strategist. "We are taking them out of their comfort zone. But the sessions give them a depth and breadth of insights and help them see their role in the world. We don't invent anything; we just connect the dots and bring the things they haven't looked at to light the way for their business."

Senior strategist Maggie Schear explains, "Our clients tell us it's the most fun, exciting, intellectually nourishing day of their careers. The neat thing is that you may be speaking with an astronomer who is sitting across the table from a philosopher—and a lot of insights come from the cross-pollination between disciplines."

We deliberately keep the conversation at a 30,000-foot level and away from the everyday language of business. A week after completing the interaction, we provide the client with a synthesis of the session that translates the philosophical insights into business strategy.

Invitations to the World's Greatest Cocktail Party

Let's say that you belong to a book club. How thrilled would you be if you could invite any three authors in the world to come to one of your meetings? Well, what if you could invite just about anyone in the world to come and spend 3 hours in a meaningful dialogue about your company?

Preparing a guest list for an incubation session is like putting together the world's greatest cocktail party, corporate style. And part of the fun is that no one ever turns down your invitation.

Luminaries come from all over the world and all walks of life, and their ages range from 9 to 90. When working on purpose for Georgia-Pacific, we invited third graders over to discuss best practices for family interaction through cleaning. "What would family paper-based cleaning products look like?" we asked. "Dust booties that slide across the floor!" screamed BrightHouse's youngest luminary.

No two luminaries are alike—other than sharing a penchant for the Aristotle equation: *"Where your talents and the needs of the world cross, there lies your vocation."* To keep our participants inspired, we have the original quotation in large letters above our conference room door.

It's like recruiting for *Mission: Impossible*. We are forming intellectual SWAT teams, like mixing the Manhattan Project with Black Mountain College with Disney Imagineers. It's similar to Plato's Academy, BrightHouse's version of Mount Olympus. It's a visit to the Oracle at Delphi.

In addition to renowned professors from top universities, we've had personal trainers, astronauts, explorers, mountain climbers, Nobel Prize–winning scientists, and even the highest-ranking nun on the planet.

VIP: Very Important Purpose

The individuals we have at our incubation sessions all provide specific insights and offer particular abilities. We'll invite a historian if we want to be able to read the future from the past. Scientists help connect observation with discovery, and philosophers can enlighten on the essence of being and knowing. We might even study ceremonial tribal drinking rituals if you want new ways of thinking about beverage consumption.

Artists, physicians, musicians, writers—just about anyone can be a valuable luminary as long as that person has a razor-sharp intellect and unfettered creativity. It's like creating a board of directors who are far from being boring or bored. In fact, the members get on board with your mission and offer a road map—direction you might not have considered that will be purposeful.

"Our luminaries have honed their crafts. Whether it's child-rearing in Samoa or blindly adventuring up Mount Everest, they bring focus and new perspectives to the process," said BrightHouse creative strategist and producer Ashley Lewis. "That's where the magic comes in—when you have so many brilliant minds in one room, pushing, pulling, and stretching each other. We often experience an aha moment, a communal epiphany during the session. But if it doesn't happen at that particular moment, it happens as a result of the session. The meeting provides the fodder for the aha moment to come later."

Banking on Luminaries

As SunTrust Bank executive vice president and chief marketing and client experience officer Rilla Delorier tells it, "We definitely experienced our aha moment. And it gave us a new perspective on how we viewed our role as a company and helped shape our thinking as we set out to make a bigger difference for our teammates, clients, communities, and shareholders." With total assets of $178 billion, SunTrust stands as one of the world's most respected institutions. But it wanted to stand for more. As Delorier explains, "We have changed our vision, our values, our people practices. We have recast our purpose, which changes how we interact with clients, how we our present our brand and our messaging platform, and how we are involved in our community."

Delorier likens the process of investigation SunTrust underwent to reveal its ethos "to uncovering three gems." She continued, "Now it was time to polish them and make them shine." These elements were trust, the tension between a large institution trying to maintain a local feel, and the sun.

We brought in a BrightHouse luminary and political scientist specializing in trust. She shared with us the insight that trust is always relational and contextual, formed through encapsulated interest. Encapsulated interest exists when our interests are wrapped up in someone else's and taken to heart.

From that insight, SunTrust learned that transparency is a crucial element of trust. It isn't just about giving and getting when dealing with clients. It's about being clear on what SunTrust is getting and giving, too.

Another BrightHouse luminary, an environmental biologist, talked about nature, where large and small life forms coexist. He shared with us a critical building block for SunTrust's purpose: the idea that nature uses dynamic creativity, turning storms into opportunities for creativity or turning predators into collaborators. For example, a tree might turn a harvest ant into an ally by ensconcing its seed in fruit that encourages the ant to spread the seed farther and wider.

"From that, we learned to adjust about how to handle threats," said Delorier. "For example, we could look at the regulatory environment as an opportunity to build a partnership and serve our clients better—rather than as an obstacle."

The major aha moment for SunTrust came from the third area: the sun. A BrightHouse luminary and one of the best-known and most widely read astronomers in the world came to teach the group about the science of the sun. He also provided one of the most shocking moments ever in a luminary session. In explaining the role of the sun, he wanted us to experience what it was like in the beginning when Greeks saw a ball of fire in the sky and had no idea what it was.

He reached into his briefcase, pulled out a book, opened it up, and flames shot out of it—3 feet into the air. In addition to causing us all to jump out of our seats with shock, it also reconnected us with the awe ancient men must have felt when they first looked at the sun.

Although that flame was quickly extinguished, the spark it ignited is changing the direction of SunTrust Bank. "We began talking about the sun and how [it allows you to] see things you don't normally see; you don't see colors without the sun," Delorier said. "That was our aha moment. SunTrust can light the path for people, helping them see things they wouldn't see with optimism and consistency. We can light the path to financial well-being. The sun also brings warmth, which is a key currency to the way we interact with our clients."

Purpose Cleans Up

Those yellow cleaning carts and mop buckets you see in malls and airports are made by Rubbermaid Commercial Products (RCP). We wanted to explore the phrase "Cleanliness is next to godliness," so we invited someone close to God: BrightHouse luminary and author of *Following the Path: The Search for a Life of Passion, Purpose, and Joy*, Sister Joan Chittister. According to Sister Joan, the aforementioned phrase "asks us whether or not we are making the best possible world for people to live in—for their health and self-esteem. It's about care for the universe that implies care for all earth's creation—animal, vegetable, mineral, human."

This thought elevated the way that RCP would think about its work. There would be no menial work from this day forward—only sacred work. Every profession, from leadership to the hard-working janitor, would be proud to wear the Rubbermaid shield logo. Sister Joan said, "To be in this business is a holy-making thing. It's not the lowest of the services that we provide. We are willing to go to any depth to take humanity to its best."

A second luminary, this one an accomplished architect and architecture professor, taught us about how the world builds and disintegrates at the same time—and why it's meaningful for RCP to be a builder. A psychology professor shared how beauty creates pleasure. Finally, Emory University professor of anthropology Bradd Shore taught us about the importance of cleanliness and order, how they are the preconditions for society to flourish. Cleanliness is a visual cue for good intention, that a space has been cared for.

The conclusion: By creating the conditions for care, RCP could further associate themselves with moral purity, beauty, perfection, truth, and order. By taking the cares of the world away, RCP sets the world up for higher-order cares such as love and healing.

Diving into Humanity

To dive deep into the topic of courage with Emory University, we brought in astronaut and world-famous cultural anthropologist Dr. Mary Catherine Bateson, and then a blind explorer who completed all seven summits. We wanted to offer their perspectives on conquering fear and how courage changed their worldviews.

We were astonished during our work with bath and kitchen product manufacturer American Standard when we learned that modern sanitation has increased the human life span by 20 years.

At a session for a feminine product for Procter & Gamble, our luminaries opened our eyes to a significant gender difference in times of stress. When stressed, rather than respond with flight or fight, women turn to one another, a reaction called tend and befriend.

A BrightHouse luminary who is expert in comic studies, superheroes, and the hero's journey gave hand and power tool accessory maker Irwin the following super advice: "Tools extend human capabilities, enabling heroic acts. You can only screw a bolt on so far before you need a wrench." Another BrightHouse luminary who is both an award-winning author and an auto mechanic shed light on the power of the trades and the prowess of those who work with their hands. And Mary Catherine Bateson told us that the use of tools led to cultural revolutions; they increased the number of people living together and created an explosion of artistic activity.

Dr. Rick Gilkey, an Emory University professor involved in neuroscience research in the Department of Psychiatry, informed us during a session for MetLife that our definitions of success are changing, with data that "show a strong shift from economic definitions of success to definitions of significance, social impact, and personal contribution as the measure of success and well-being."

It's fascinating to note that as a result of these sessions, our clients always learn that their business can be more than a seller and server; in essence, they can be healers. As BrightHouse luminary, world-renowned philosopher, and author Dr. Sam Keen, said, "The concept that doing business without any sense of purpose can yield society or mankind any happiness is an illusion."

Dr. Keen was a part of one of my favorite BrightHouse stories, one I'll never forget. After working with Newell Rubbermaid for months on their Master Idea, we had a meeting to present our work to the company's president and chief executive officer (CEO) at the time, Mark Ketchum. He is the ultimate CEO type—very metrics oriented.

I had brought Dr. Keen as a luminary, as I often do at these type meetings.

We discussed our findings for nearly 6 hours. At the end of the lengthy session, Ketchum turns to Dr. Keen and says, "Dr. Keen, tell me really. What happens if we don't do this work?"

The noted author of 14 books on philosophy and religion with graduate degrees from Harvard and Princeton looked at Ketchum and said, "You will lose your soul." The CEO opted for purpose and a lasting legacy.

Lead Characters in Your Story of Purpose

No idea is an island unto itself. No one thought is the sole answer to the future of business. Collectively, when great minds and insight unite, we bring to light the past, the present, and the future. They merge together to create something larger than life—a way to enlarge itself with something more meaningful.

"While luminaries provide gems, ultimately, it is in the polishing and mounting—the synthesis of these nuggets— that the relevance to your brand emerges," says BrightHouse chief strategy officer, Dolly Meese.

What Is the Purpose of This Chapter?

- Incubation is about expanding our thinking about the role your brand can play in the world.
- When it comes to thinking, quantity of time is the new quality time.

- Luminaries don't help you sell; they help you tell your story of purpose.

Purpose Pointers

- Bring in luminaries to shed a billion-watt light on your brand's role in the world.
- Orchestrate the environment for incubation, not the conversation.
- Listen with the intent of being influenced.

11

Illumination

Great ideas don't appear, they evolve.

—Joey Reiman,
Thinking for a Living

The story of illumination dates back to ancient civilizations. In 275 BC, a young general named Hiero was chosen for the crown of the ancient Greek city of Syracuse. Recognizing his success as a gift from the gods, he knew he would return the favor by creating a golden crown for them. Hiero weighed out a precise amount of gold and commissioned a goldsmith to forge his gift.

The crown was delivered to Hiero. Although it seemed to be the exact weight of the provided gold, Hiero heard rumors that the goldsmith did not make the crown out of pure gold, but rather, mixed it with silver. Hiero was understandably angry and decided to get to the bottom of it.

He turned to his cousin Archimedes to solve the mystery. Renowned for his work in mathematics and physics, Archimedes spent days pondering how he could discover the truth. Deep in thought, he walked to the bathhouse for his daily bath.

As he lowered his body into the water for his last rinse, he noticed the water began to spill over the tub. Curious, he began to lower himself into the tub again and again, noticing the lower his body went, the more the water spilled over the sides of the tub.

In a moment of illumination, Archimedes realized he found the solution to Hiero's issue. Excited by his discovery, he jumped out of the tub and ran through the town naked, yelling, "Eureka, Eureka"—Greek for "I have found it! I have found it!"[1]

Investigating and incubating in a bathtub led to the illumination of how to measure volumetric weight and the indictment of the goldsmith. Although your moment of realization might not lead to such extreme behavior, it should be every bit as thrilling.

How to Have a Eureka Moment

Moments of illumination work the same way in business. After bathing in thought—incubation—you have a flash that prompts you to see something that had previously been in the dark. If the idea is bright enough, you have a Eureka moment. You cannot demand flashes of brilliance like these; you simply have to be open to them. That's all you can do. Creativity depends on what you are thinking, whom you are thinking with, and where you are thinking.

BrightHouse conducts four 3-hour ideation sessions over one month to articulate the Master Idea and narrative based on investigation and incubation insights. We hold these sessions only during the morning hours, because that's when our minds are freshest. When you combine your learning from investigation and incubation, you have everything you need to illuminate your way to a Master Idea.

To have that Eureka moment, we need to remember Archimedes' mentor Aristotle, who found purpose at the intersection of our unique gifts and the needs of the world, or in BrightHouse language, the intersection of investigation and incubation. This is also the place to start crafting your purpose statement or Master Idea.

As we first discussed in Chapter 3, your Master Idea is the fruit that has grown from the roots of your organization. It fulfills a fundamental desire in all of us. It's timeless, teaches, fulfills, is a battle cry, is ethotic, is transformative, inspires, and is born not from data but from absolute conviction. We can shout it at the top of our lungs for all to hear, yet at the same time, its whispers to our hearts. Your Master Idea is the pulse of the workplace.

Collaboration Creates More Light

Thoughtful collaboration will position your mind to reach Illumination—the euphoric moment when the lightbulb appears atop your head and shines so bright those around must look away. Master Ideas are built by teams. So let's take the time to elaborate on how to collaborate. The mindset for teamwork is one that is stitched from the threads of innocence, curiosity, and compassion. These three threads combine to cultivate collaboration. When we weave these together during team ideations, we optimize the opportunity for illumination.

Thread 1: Innocence

Innocence is not naiveté. Rather it is an openness to learn. As a child, you welcomed new ideas and teachings with an unguarded mind. This is a time to revert back to that innocence of your youth, hungry to acquire and absorb. By the time we hit middle school, we are *de-geniused*. Only a return to innocence will unearth creativity. Here's how to bring it back:

- Come into the ideation with the intention of being influenced.
- Forget your personal strategy and focus on the future.
- Say something that might be embarrassing. It's probably the big idea.

Thread 2: Curiosity

A sense of wonder is an important step toward discovery. Knowing how to wonder is the key to unlocking wonder! Contemplation leads to revelation, so you will want to be thinking before your session. Remember, the tortoise always beats the harebrained. If you want to get there first, slow down and take the time to be curious.

Here's how to do just that:

- Spend more time doing research before the meeting.
- Keep a journal by your head, not your bed. Always carry something you can make notes in.
- Ask *why* wherever you go. Be a "whys guy." When BrightHouse excavates a brand's purpose, our team works to uncover universal human truths that define consumer needs, and hence, the meaningful role the brand can play in the world. One way we do this is through constant questioning. BrightHouse's chief strategy officer, Dolly Meese, explains, "Even when we feel we've gotten to the heart of an organization's purpose, we continue to push, always asking, 'Why?' until we can ask why no longer."

Thread 3: Compassion

Compassion is a virtue that allows us to feel the hurt or distress of others. So we enter into an ideation with empathy for all stakeholders. Let your heart guide you. Because although your heart beats 2.5 billion times in your life, its real strength is its capacity for compassion. Business guru and author of *Organizing Genius*, Warren Bennis, says, "Whether they are trying to get their candidate into the White House or trying to save the free world, Great Groups always believe that they are doing something vital, even holy."[2]

How do you ideate with compassion?

- Pick an enemy, not a competitor, to knock off. An enemy is something that threatens living things and the planet, not the marketplace.
- Put yourselves in your stakeholders' shoes to get outside your box.
- Make good the goal.

The Result: Collaboration

Your team's innocence, curiosity, and compassion are necessary for genuine collaboration. Teams win because there are more arms, legs, eyes, mouths, brains, and hearts. Also, they can move faster and more efficiently. Collaboration is like making a good soup: the only way to create an intense depth of flavor is through fine ingredients and time. And there is no way to fake or replicate it. Just as it takes numerous vegetables and meats to produce a tasty base for your soup, it takes an abundance of collaborative minds and time to form a Master Idea.

Michelangelo had a team of 13 artists who painted the Sistine Chapel. Six hundred fifty artists worked on Walt

Disney's *Fantasia*. And almost 1 million people constructed the Great Wall of China. Truly great accomplishments happen only when people come together and work together for a common purpose.

Places to Think

Thinking is not a core competency in business. Daydreaming is frowned upon, and fast solutions are rewarded. As a result, the workplace is often the *last* place you'll find real live thinkers.

Ideas don't like offices, and no insights come from off-sites. The time has come to think outside those boxes. Despite the fact that creativity is any unconditioned response, we can still work on developing the conditions for optimal billion-watt thinking.

My Five Favorite Places for Illumination:

1. *The car*. Turn off the phone and turn on those wheels in your brain. As someone who is paid for his big ideas, I think of MPG as millions per gallon. The car might seem like a strange place to think; however, we are relaxed and alert when we're on the road. Our brains are geared for this neutral mode, and ideas start popping up everywhere. Think of stoplights as the gifts that let you write down those thoughts.

2. *The shower*. The shower is a place of wonder. It's an enclosed, private, warm place with great sound—in essence, a womb for ideas! And that's why so many come to us while we're in the shower. Think about it: I bet you can remember at least one time (probably more) where you experienced a moment of inspiration

in the shower. I actually installed a shower in my office with the letters T-H-I-N-K etched in five tiles. And as Archimedes found, baths work too. Here we are not doing or saying anything. We're just being.

3. *The john.* Rodin's famous statue *The Thinker* assumed the position for good reason. Sitting on the john is a time of release in more ways than one or two. This can be a time for deep contemplation rather than just a waste. The john is an entertainment venue for the mind. There is always reading material. In fact, 74 percent of people read on the toilet, according to Quilted Northern's 2004 Bathroom Confidential Study.[3]

4. *The park.* Unfortunately, many of us have NDD— nature deficit disorder. But nature has all the big ideas. Imagination was born here. Get outside your head and head outside.

5. *Places of worship.* Despite the fact that I was born Jewish, I go to different places of worship when I need a big idea. Nothing beats divine inspiration; the architecture surrounding you is built on the idea of getting as close to the heavens as humanly possible.

All of these places are idea-friendly. They are sanctuaries where private ideations can be held between you and all that has been and might be. Ironically, these places of quietude are where ideas can be heard the loudest.

Now that you have read mine, what are your favorite places to think?

We all have unique ways and places for finding illumination. As a kid, my mother demanded that I see a movie the night before a test. The result was better grades back then and better ideas today. What do you do to stimulate *your* imagination? The great thinkers all had something—or somewhere—unique:

- Writer Ralph Waldo Emerson would check into a hotel room.
- Philosopher Friedrich Nietzsche would take long walks.
- Great artist Leonardo Da Vinci would stare at cracks in the wall.

A four-sided box made out of steel, aluminum, copper, glass, and vinyl was the colony dish for some of the biggest thinkers on the planet. Disney, Hewlett-Packard, and Apple started in garages, which only serves as proof that the biggest piece of real estate on the planet is your brain.

Minds at Work

Not only do you have to change your mind-set to illuminate your brand, but you must also change your language. Any alteration—anything that makes your daily "grind" just a little bit different—can have an impact:

- Change your routine.
- Change your office.
- Change your direction.
- Then, change your mind.
- Just *change*.

The language of illumination is a change in how you think about and view the controlling principles. We all hear the same "idea killers" again and again in the workplace. It is now time to rethink how we express ourselves and turn these idea killers into idea *creators*.

Consider the following opposing mind-sets and phrases:

Idea Killer	Idea Creator
It can't be done.	It's never been done before.
It's not in the budget.	We'll find the money.
Impossible.	I'm possible.
Don't waste my time.	I'll find the time.
This is my last try.	Let's try one more time.
Rolling eyeballs.	Laser focus.
Sighing.	Surprising!

Never shake your head at people's ideas. No one, no matter what his or her level of "expertise," is in a position to judge the merits of an idea whose time has not come. It's a tragedy to think of the many brilliant thoughts that were slaughtered by a wince, a frown, a sigh, or rolling eyeballs. Cynicism is the enemy of creativity. Ideas are born drowning, so make it a point to save one every day. It, in turn, might be the one that saves your company—or the world.

However, you have to change your mind in order to do this—so that you can change the world. We cannot become who we need to be by remaining who we are, individually or as organizations. Reformatting your mind to think in a different type of way plays a vital role in reaching illumination. The manner in which you think is as important as what you find in thought.

- **There are no rules**. There are no guidelines, structure, direction, laws, principles, or procedures when it comes to illuminating; it is a free-flowing process without boundaries. As great thinker Thomas Edison said: "There ain't no rules around here, we are trying to accomplish something."[4] There are rule makers, rule takers, and rule breakers. Rule makers are lawyers. Rule takers are traditional managers. Rule breakers are the artists and scholars. Don't just respect rules; *inspect* rules. They may be limiting your creativity as much as anything else. In fact, the imagination rules!

- **Turn on your senses**. Your imagination is the organ of meaning; it has five parts called *senses*. Eyes are for seeing your work in a new light. Ears are for listening twice as hard. The fact that there are two of them but you have only one mouth should tell you something. BrightHouse has an open floor plan and open-air deck. With no walls, we hear, see, and feel the air and can even reach out to our thought partners for help. Our kitchen is filled with food for thought as well. Our snacks include blueberries, soybeans, nuts, pumpkin seeds, chocolate, and whole grain cereals for breakfast and, of course, organic coffee. Business underestimates how important our senses are. The bottom line is that many senses create dollars.

- **Routinization is the enemy of innovation**. Over time, the groove becomes a rut and then a grave for great ideas. Routines are for gymnasts, not luminaries. I have yet to find the definition for the human limit in the dictionary. The goal of your effort is to move the impossible to the improbable to the imminent. Instead of "Why?" it is time to start asking, "Why *not?*"

- **Move from wonder? to wonder!** Curiosity, innocence, aliveness—some would call these our child-like traits.

We say they are the key ingredients for mature learning and discovery, for revelation and awe. It's the magic that changes the minds of the people who can change the world. To be a luminary is to be a beacon and lead society in its unquenchable desire to be astonished. All great ideas were deemed absurd at first. They are also the ones that last. The emotion aroused by something awe-inspiring, astounding, or marvelous is the fabric of wonder.

• **Sleep on it**. As filmmaker Steven Spielberg said, "I dream for a living."[5] Mediocrity is self-inflicted; genius is self-bestowed. Whatever you are when you wake up is who you are until you go to sleep. So think big, do it big, say it big, or stay under the blanket.

Illumination Is Magic

Illumination is about magic and transformation. One of my favorite books is *The Alchemist*, authored by Paulo Coelho in 1988. Alchemists believed that at a certain high temperature metals would free themselves of individual properties, allowing the soul of the world to be freed. They called the discovery the "Master Work."

Every chemical reaction transforms the elements involved into something new. Illumination works the same way. It takes the materials of investigation and incubation and transforms them into a new and illuminating insight.

Like alchemy or chemistry, illumination is about transforming a collection of ideas and information into a tangible and meaningful Master Idea, one that's driven by purpose and articulated authentically. It is about believing the time you spent investigating and incubating will come together in a remarkable and sparkling way. It is the culmination of your hard work, noble intentions, and dedication to the collaborative process.

Illumination is where what your company offers the world intersects and aligns with what the world needs from your company. It is time to join a new way of working in business, where the creative mind is revered in a world of less analytics and more alchemy.

The Master Idea is your truth. Discovered, articulated, and activated, it guides and inspires your company. Illumination is the light that lets people dream in daylight. It is what Archimedes found in the bathtub and the idea I want to shower you with in this book.

Articulating Your Master Idea

What did John F. Kennedy's, Franklin Delano Roosevelt's, and Abraham Lincoln's inaugural addresses have in common? Each had a Master Idea that embodied a higher ideal. For Kennedy, it was "Ask not what your country can do for you—ask what you can do for your country." It's the equivalent of Roosevelt's "The only thing we have to fear is fear itself," and Lincoln's "With malice toward none, with charity for all...."

Now you don't have to be a speechwriter, but you will have to know how to put words together so that they make it through the Master Idea criteria. This is one of the values at BrightHouse, eloquence. Or as our chief creative officer, Cathy Carlisi, says, "The sound and rhythm of words matter as much as the meaning. They are what cause people to remember a phrase and enjoy repeating it. For that phrase to come alive."

Here are rules to remember:

- **Choose the right words**. Write something everyone knows but that no one has ever heard before, like Graco's "Cradle those who cradle them."

- **Make the words play**. We have all heard of word play. Well this is vocabulary's playground. Mix and match industry-specific words with human truths, and you will get Paper Mate's "Our hearts make the world write."

- **Can you chisel them in stone?** Although Master Ideas may be playful, they are not here to play around. They must possess gravitas and power, like Irwin's "All guts, all glory."

- **Combine know-how with wow**. It's your company's or brand's uniqueness plus the wow you are bringing to the world. It's your point plus poetry, it's intelligence plus eloquence, it's precise but tells your story of purpose, like Graco's "Cradle those who cradle them." As the Hopi Indian tribe contends, "the one who tells the story rules the world."

Use the Venn Diagrams to Craft Your Purpose

Try this exercise after your investigation and incubation (see Figure 11.1 and Figure 11.2). On the left side of the Venn diagram write down some initial thoughts regarding the unique talents of the brand. On the right side, write down the needs of the world. At the intersection of the two, what expression would you create that communicates your Master Idea?

Write down some initial Master Ideas. Then check them against the listed criteria (Figure 11.3).

What Is the Purpose of This Chapter?

- Illumination is the intersection of your unique talents and the needs of the world.

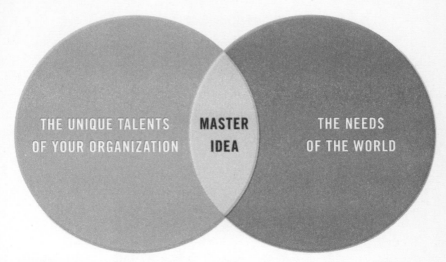

FIGURE 11.1 The BrightHouse Purpose Intersection Venn Diagram
Source: © BrightHouse. Illustration by David Paprocki.

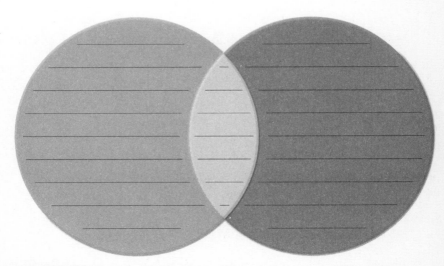

FIGURE 11.2 The BrightHouse Purpose Intersection Venn Diagram
Workbook
Source: © BrightHouse. Illustration by David Paprocki.

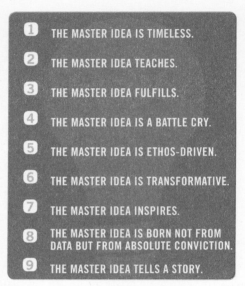

1. THE MASTER IDEA IS TIMELESS.

2. THE MASTER IDEA TEACHES.

3. THE MASTER IDEA FULFILLS.

4. THE MASTER IDEA IS A BATTLE CRY.

5. THE MASTER IDEA IS ETHOS-DRIVEN.

6. THE MASTER IDEA IS TRANSFORMATIVE.

7. THE MASTER IDEA INSPIRES.

8. THE MASTER IDEA IS BORN NOT FROM DATA BUT FROM ABSOLUTE CONVICTION.

9. THE MASTER IDEA TELLS A STORY.

FIGURE 11.3   BrightHouse Principles of a Master Idea
Source: © BrightHouse. Illustration by David Paprocki.

- Compassion leads to collaboration, collaboration leads to illumination.
- The manner in which you think is as important as what you find in thought.

Purpose Pointers

- Choose your words *why*sly.
- Create a Master Idea that inspires, guides, and heals.
- Remember to make the Master Idea memorable.

12

Illustration

Lights, camera, actions!

—Joey Reiman,
on activating purpose

Illustration is how you bring your Master Idea to life for all those who will live it. "We shall overcome" is an incredibly powerful Master Idea. It became tangible and real for the world when houses of worship opened their doors with the message for people to open their hearts.

For many who could not read, stained glass windows told a grand story of purpose. And song invited you to be a verse in that story. This illustration of a Master Idea would change the way we live and think, forever. Illustration amplifies and communicates the Master Idea through carefully selected words, pictures, and music that *astonish*.

Truth in Advertising

When Nike said "Just Do It," it gave voice to the belief that humans have no limits—at least in the realm of sports.

Disney was founded on the Master Idea that it is possible to make dreams come true, articulated by Jiminy Cricket's "When you wish upon a star, it makes no difference who you are."[1]

TV spoke to the heart of Gen X when it put forth the notion that free expression is a human right and proclaimed it with the battle cry, "I Want My MTV!"

Figure 12.1 shows a few examples of Master Ideas and the purposeful articulations they inspired.

Apple's tagline that captures their Master Idea—"Think different"—is no less a movement in that it gives permission to artists who would otherwise have no flag to raise in the battleground of the business world. Using Alfred Hitchcock, Lucy and Ricky Ricardo, Jim Henson, Muhammad Ali, and Miles Davis as creative role models, Apple launched a creative revolution.

Movements begin with a small group of inspired souls who emerge, find one another, and share their private

FIGURE 12.1 Human Truths and Articulations

Source: © BrightHouse. Illustration by David Paprocki.

Illustration **163**

dilemmas—and in doing, create a public issue. Civil rights, women's suffrage, and even freedom itself were all movements incited by Master Ideas. "This idea arose in the minds of a few morally impassioned thinkers," says Cal State East Bay professor Theodore Roszak.[2]

Master Ideas Are *Not* Slogans

The best advertising is driven by human truths called Master Ideas. Although this is not the case with most brands, I meet business leaders who are actively seeking a way to develop better brands and brighter companies every single day. And they are turning to the power of purpose. Slogans inspired by Master Ideas resonate more deeply, both inside and outside the organization. For example, "Whole Foods, Whole People, Whole Planet" is not just a tagline for Whole Foods Market; it's an operating philosophy that calls for interdependence.[3] Whole Foods produce is an offering from organic farmers around the world, its staff is diverse, and the planet is as important a stakeholder as its customers.

Be It, Do It, Say It

Today, purpose without action is useless. Although every organization has its own version of how it develops its go-to-market strategy, at BrightHouse, we use our proven framework of *Be-Do-Say* to activate and implement an organization's Master Idea. *Be-Do-Say* impacts not only how an organization goes to market to create more powerful relationships with external stakeholders, such as customers, consumers, and partners, but also with internal stakeholders, including employees and shareholders. The Four I's

INVESTIGATION
- EXCAVATE THE BRAND'S ETHOS TO DEFINE ITS UNIQUE AND AUTHENTIC VALUES.
- PREPARE AND DELIVER INVESTIGATION SYNTHESIS, INCLUDING ETHOS-DRIVEN THEMES.

INCUBATION
- UNDERSTAND THE MEANINGFUL ROLE THE BRAND PLAYS IN THE WORLD.
- CONDUCT LUMINARY INTERACTION WORKSHOP TO PUSH THINKING ON THE ROLE THE BRAND CAN PLAY IN THE WORLD.
- PREPARE AND DELIVER INCUBATION SYNTHESIS, INCLUDING KEY LUMINARY INSIGHTS.

ILLUMINATION
- ARTICULATE THE UNIQUE INTERSECTION OF THE BRAND ETHOS AND VALUES WITH ITS ROLE IN THE WORLD — THE MASTER IDEA.
- CRAFT THE MASTER IDEA ARTICULATION AND NARRATIVE.

ILLUSTRATION
- BRING THE MASTER IDEA TO LIFE THROUGH FILM.
- CONDUCT INTERNAL IDEATIONS TO CREATE CONCEPTS FOR INTERNAL AND EXTERNAL AUDIENCE THROUGH THE BE-DO-SAY FRAMEWORK:

BE
- ENGAGED EMPLOYEES — PURPOSE-INFUSED CONCEPTS FOR ORGANIZATIONAL AND HR STRATEGIES

DO
- ALIGNED AND INSPIRED BEHAVIOR — PURPOSE-INFUSED CONCEPTS FOR INNOVATION, PARTNERSHIPS, DIGITAL COMMUNITIES, AND PURPOSE-DRIVEN ACTION

SAY
- PURPOSE-DRIVEN COMMUNICATION FOR EXTERNAL AUDIENCES — PURPOSE-INSPIRED TRADITIONAL AND NONTRADITIONAL MESSAGING AND MEDIA

FIGURE 12.2　The BrightHouse Four I's Ideation Process and *Be-Do-Say*

Source: © BrightHouse. Illustration by David Paprocki.

Illustration **165**

(investigation, incubation, illumination, and illustration) get you to *why*, and *Be-Do-Say* tells you *how* (See Figure 12.2). It ensures our people and actions are constantly and consistently delivering on the purpose.

- *Be* engages your associates with purpose.
- *Do* brings purposeful actions to your company and people every day.
- *Say* communicates purposeful messaging to all stakeholders.

Be Is Who You Are

How many people in your company can truly be who they are? *Be* encourages managers to let their employees bring their whole selves to work, embrace their values, and join a movement. From onboarding to transitioning, *Be* employs company values in service of a healthy culture—and answers crucial questions such as:

- How does purpose impact our behaviors every day?
- What are our shared beliefs?
- What is the fabric of our ethos?
- What guiding beliefs and ideals characterize our community?

Be Hammers It Home for Irwin

Take Irwin Tools, for example. Irwin makes tools used by hands all around the world. Considering the Master Idea of "All guts, all glory," we suggested that Irwin chisel the following industry-specific, memorable, and directive values into the rungs of a ladder in their lobby, so that all may see them every day:

- **Have bolder, meet older.** We have a youthful spirit and a hunger to improve and to win, along with a long history of well-known products.

- **Be tough as nails.** We have had to bend through a history of changes, but we have never broken.
- **Be true blue.** Our tools are tried and true and never let our end users down on the job.
- **Build with those who build.** We have a curiosity and an obsession with our end users, because we are end users ourselves.
- **Make every little bit count.** We know how to bring individual tools together to create innovative solutions.

Be Is the Recipe for Calphalon

When working with Calphalon, a brand of cookware products from Newell Rubbermaid, we developed five key ingredients for ethotic alignment:

- **The business of life:** The passion for life and for Calphalon is based on good company and great experiences together.
- **Love made:** It is the result of ingredients, people, and ideas coming together; it is a labor of love.
- **The Calphalon gut:** The organization is elevated through collective intuition.
- **The host at the table:** There is a comfort in bringing people and ideas together.
- **Approachable innovation:** Remain the approachable expert with an appreciation for living life fully.

Illustration **167**

Calphalon values were engraved on measuring spoons and handed out to associates to remind them of Calphalon's "Measures of Success." Employees live these tenets every day, ensuring that the Calphalon spirit always remains intact as the company grows and changes.

Do Is Living Your *Why* Through Actions

Be is who you are. *Do* is what you do with it. *Do* aligns and inspires actions. *Do* develops tools and resources for bringing your company's purpose to life. Through designing high-level strategy and tactical plans for activating your Master Idea both internally and externally, you can create acts on purpose for internal associates.

Do emphasizes the answers to questions like:

- How do our actions bring our purpose to life?
- How do our tools and resources bring our purpose to life?
- How can we implement new and unique programs both externally and internally?
- How do we connect with the consumer in an interactive and meaningful manner?

Do Is the Write Stuff for Paper Mate

"Our hearts make the world write" is the Master Idea for Newell Rubbermaid's Paper Mate brand.

Do is about inventing ways to positively affect your company and the world through unique programs, products, and services. Penny McIntyre, president of Newell Rubbermaid's Consumer Group, said, "I think our purpose provides a common language and point of commitment for the organization to rally around. It speaks to the more fundamental element of why we do what we do—how we see our personal pride being invested in what we spend a tremendous amount of time doing . . . work. It is a tool for retention of our associates as well as a differentiator from other businesses. Purpose provides the *why* and *how* to the *what* we do every day."

To McIntyre's point, Paper Mate might have said, "We exist to connect more people through our pens." But "Our hearts make the world write" is a truth incorporating their ethos and their logo, two hearts. To bring their purpose to life, McIntyre and the Paper Mate team took action to send pens to children in Malawi, giving them the opportunity to make the world 'write' through education.

Purpose Cuts Through

Lenox Industrial Tools took one of their values—"Go the extra mile"—to the races. The value states: "We go for great, not good. We rally around any challenge, turn trial into triumph. We do not accept compromise, shortcuts, or defeat. We keep going until we find a solution that grows our success, our customers' success and our ability to shape our world."

Lenox sponsored the New Hampshire Motor Speedway NASCAR Race, the Lenox 300. They convinced NASCAR to add an extra mile and changed the name to the Lenox 301 based on their value of "going the extra mile."

They also sent out a call for the Extra Mile Hero, an award for going over and above in an act of service to others, as well as using the Lenox products in their work with integrity. Lenox received more than 600 entries for the Extra Mile Hero award and brought the 10 finalists to the New Hampshire race to await the big announcement given by Jeff Burton. If the Lenox driver won, the Extra Mile Hero would win $1 million to split with the charity of his or her choice.

Illustration **169**

A Bicycle Built for 20 Million

On a recent trip to BrightHouse Brasil, I was asked to give my own "Story of Purpose" speech to the leadership of a bank. I learned that the bank also had a purpose. And the way they demonstrated it blew me away.

Andrea Cordeiro Pinotti is head of institutional marketing at Banco Itaú, the largest private bank in the southern hemisphere, according to Bloomberg on December 31, 2011. The bank's purpose is "to be an agent of transformation." Cordeiro Pinotti said, "To do so we have to go beyond our role as a financial institution." So how do they do it? With bicycles! As Cordeiro Pinotti explains, "Rio de Janeiro and São Paulo are two of the most important and largest cities in Brasil. Urban mobility has been a big problem for both cities, since they have grown tremendously over the past years and traffic has gotten only heavier, which impacts people's quality of life."

"With this project, we not only give people an alternative means of transportation—and transform the way they move across the city—we also give them an eco-friendly way to enjoy their own cities. And they appreciate it a lot."

Here's how it works:

The person goes to one of the bank's bike stations to release the bike. That person can either call the service central or can download an app to his or her cell phone and make the reservation personally. According to Cordeiro Pinotti, "Most people tell us they love it!"

I know I did. My wife and I picked up two bicycles and rode the Copacabana. As Cordeiro Pinotti explains, "It brings people closer to our brand. The response we get through social media is huge. People take pictures of themselves riding the bikes, they make movies, and they send us messages. Many people want to *buy* the bicycles. But unfortunately, they're not for sale."

Saying it with purpose opens the doors to thinking beyond conventional media such as TV, radio, print, and outdoor advertising. In fact, the best way to say it is to go to the movies.

Purpose Puts the Pop in Popcorn

People love going to the movies. The experience brings people into a story that teaches, inspires, and guides along the way. By literally capturing life as we experience it—with words, images, ambient sound, and music—film can inspire and communicate with emotion as no other medium can.

Now it's time for you to make a Master Idea film, just as we do for every client who seeks purpose. When the journey is done, it's the best way to debut purpose for the organization.

The Master Idea film is a visual expression of your Master Idea. Its job is to take your narrative and make a short—but *powerful*—film on it. A Master Idea film brings a company's purpose to life. Call it *visual strategy* or the emotional complement to the rational strategy presented in the project's deck. The Master Idea film is meant to be used for internal purposes. It captures the essence of a company's purpose in a way that allows employees throughout the organization to understand and become galvanized by that sentiment.

A little on my own ethos: After graduating from Brandeis University, I boarded the ocean liner Leonardo Da Vinci and sailed to Genoa. I then drove to Cinecittà Studios in Rome, Italy, to intern with Italian movie director Federico Fellini. Fellini is considered one of the most influential filmmakers of the twentieth century and won five Academy Awards. I learned from Fellini's 40-year career in the movies that if you want people to remember something,

Illustration   **171**

you better create an emotional experience around it—and nothing does that better than a purpose film. Following is a script written by our chief creative officer and nationally recognized poet, Cathy Carlisi, from our film called *The Purpose of Purpose*:

(The film opens with a quote from Gandhi.)
    A small body of determined spirits fired by an unquenchable faith in their mission can alter the course of history.
    (Then in bold and beautiful type. . .)
    Purpose is not The What
    The Where or The Who
    Purpose is The Why.
    (Pictures of Jimmy Carter, Eileen Collins, the founder of Google, and Mother Teresa flash by.)
    It's why we struggle.
    It's why we strive.
    It's why we exist.
    Purpose helps us wake.
    Work. Purpose helps us sleep at night.
    King called it Freedom.
    Kennedy called it the Moon.
    Disney called it Magic.
    (Black and white pictures of King, Kennedy, and Disney appear.)
    Magic that creates movements
    That create movement.
    (Close-up photos of the faces of Ted Turner, Paul Newman, and Maya Angelou flash across the screen.)
    The purpose of Purpose
    Is to generate Energy
    (A breathtaking picture of Martha Graham.)
    Ballistic Momentum
    A force that drives you
    Like an athlete
    (Muhammad Ali training and Michael Jordan in flight.)

Like a warrior
The purpose of Purpose
is to fulfill a fundamental human desire
(Loved ones embracing one another.)
to transform
to grow wings
(A Southwest airplane in flight appears.)
to defy gravity.
(An astronaut in space is shown.)
PURPOSE: to stretch out
(Alvin Ailey dancers with their hands in the sky.)
to strain
to lean towards something
Something that makes you feel so alive
Like a bloodhound with his head out the
car window
(A picture of Steve Jobs.)
Apple calls it creativity.
Nike calls it human potential.
Whole Foods calls it the planet.
(A picture of a man picking a vegetable from the earth.)
The purpose of Purpose
Is to be part of something bigger
*(A group of hands, one bigger than the next, on top of
one another.)*
to restore
(Barack Obama speaking.)
to guide
(An image of Winston Churchill.)
to inspire
(A picture of the Dalai Lama, rosaries in hand.)
to move beyond success
to significance
(Nelson Mandela looking out the window.)
to a satisfaction so deep
it can only come from knowing
that what you do matters,
that the work you do
(A picture of a father swinging his smiling child around.)

Illustration 173

(Pictures of family members sharing joy.)
CAN
WILL
Change the world.

As Carlisi says, this film employs "the eloquence needed to stop thinking and start feeling." Your film needs to do the same, but in your unique voice.

Your Master Idea film is the visual story of your purpose. It's your company's soul in a bottle. Your film is sure to astonish when its story is relevant to your company and the world—and created with unexpected words and pictures. Make sure you have plenty of popcorn.

Be authentic, *do* things that show you mean it, and *say* it the right way. Do this and you will have bigger outcomes and incomes. Illustration is the time to show the world your vision forged and sculpted from the rock solid pillars of your ethos, culture, and values.

What Is the Purpose of This Chapter?

- Illustrating the Master Idea creates alignment and advocacy internally and externally for all stakeholders.
- Activation is an inside-outside job. Start with *Be*, then *Do*, then *Say*, not the other way around.
- Master Idea Illustration is words, pictures, and music that astonish.

Purpose Pointers

- First, *be* who you are.
- Second, *do* it every day in every way.
- And third, *say* it publicly.

You have just completed the Four I's Ideation Process to arrive at your purpose and see how the Be-Do-Say framework activates purpose. My hope is that you now have an idea of your Master Idea, values, and narrative to start telling your story of purpose.

Of course, this is but an overview. More than likely, you will want to talk more with your leadership associates and your own luminaries. Be patient. The BrightHouse Four I's Ideation Process typically takes 16 weeks, and activation through the Be-Do-Say framework is a daily ongoing practice.

My recommendation is that you put together your own Purpose, Inc., a small group of people who will take the time and effort necessary to complete each step more thoroughly. In the end you will have unearthed your ethos and used your culture to build purpose-driven values that influence your strategies and tactics.

Most important, you will have a better brand and a brighter company and will have joined the ranks of those who are writing a new and powerful narrative for business.

IV

Creating a Lasting Legacy

Business has only one real customer: society.

—Joey Reiman,
on the future of business

For the first time in history, business is everywhere, therefore putting it in the venerable position of elevating its role in society. Business's commitment to work with greater purpose will create better brands, brighter companies, and lasting legacies.

A grand inheritance will come from companies of meaning that will make enhanced goods more available to more people. Many US multinationals are already bigger than some countries and can help provide capital and infrastructure for emerging societies. But as you will read in Part IV, there are more than 4 billion underserved people living below those emerging markets.

A vanguard of purposeful leaders and companies driven by noble cause are already reaching out to achieve noble goals: eradicate poverty and hunger, ensure primary education, promote gender equality, reduce childhood mortality, improve maternal health, guarantee environmental sustainability, and rid the world of disease.

Best-selling author and speaker Malcolm Gladwell thinks that Bill Gates will be remembered and Steve Jobs will be forgotten—because Gates's philanthropic work makes him an anomaly in the entrepreneurial world.

Only team effort among businesses and brands can mitigate the ills of society and create a world as idyllic as Camelot, a mythical and legendary place we will visit next.

I am reminded of the purpose work for the nonprofit organization the United Way. Their ethos tells the story of four religious leaders from different faiths who came together to console and rebuild Atlanta after a devastating snowstorm a century ago. The Master Idea that I penned from this story is "Only everyone." Their most recent advertising campaign followed: "LIVE UNITED." In this spirit, we must work united as well, for only in doing so we will achieve the *why* behind purpose.

Part IV reveals *why* and brings your story of purpose to its next chapter. How will you choose to do business in the future? Will it be "business as usual"? Or will you join the ranks of the mighty who believe that the life of one's business should better the business of life?

A world on purpose is a herculean promise that will bring business back for good and the world back to great.

13

The Road to Camelot

In short, there's simply not
A more congenial spot
For Happily-Ever-Aftering
Than Here in Camelot.

—Alan Jay Lerner,
lyricist[1]

As many of us are aware, Camelot is the stuff of legend. Made famous by twelfth-century legends of King Arthur, lyricist Alan Jay Lerner's 1960 hit musical, and President John F. Kennedy's wildly admired administration by the same name, *Camelot* today has simply come to mean a place or time of idyllic happiness.

For business, it can be a real destination where organizations of meaning bring both goods and good to the world. Camelot companies and brands have created their own mythologies by their benevolence and goodwill. These organizations were born with great purpose and garner the love of their associates, customers, partners, and shareholders. Of course, many organizations are still seeking Camelot after having lost what made them extraordinary in the first place.

The Journey to Camelot

For purposes of identifying corporate purpose, BrightHouse, along with Emory University business dean Andrea Hershatter, created a visual framework that positions and classifies organizations along a vertical and a horizontal axis.

The worn path takes us east, in the direction of operational excellence. More purposeful brands move along a new path toward soulful excellence and a brighter company. Purpose-bound organizations use the graph shown in Figure 13.1 as a benchmark for where they are on the road to Camelot.

Let's break down the components of this matrix and discuss each with a bit more detail.

Operational Excellence (The *X*-Axis)

Operational excellence is generally a measure of an organization's performance. It is required to execute efficiently in alignment with strategic imperatives in order for a company to survive in the corporate arena. This axis maps the return on resources relative to key competitors. Since this indicates how effectively the organization uses its resources—and its ability to deliver consistent value to the consumer—we have labeled the horizontal axis *operational excellence*.

Soulful Excellence (The *Y*-Axis)

Soulful excellence is a measure of a company's purpose. Companies situated high on the vertical or *"why"*-axis are distinctive and fully alive. Associates are highly engaged. Ideals, values, and objectives are aligned to serve all stakeholders, and authenticity reigns. In a world that is demanding more meaning from business, this new measure recognizes

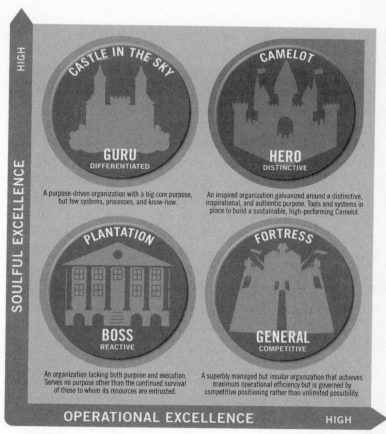

FIGURE 13.1 Camelot Matrix

Source: © BrightHouse. Illustration by David Paprocki.

noble intention and contribution as yardsticks. Hence, we have labeled the vertical axis *soulful excellence*.

Camelot: The Best of Both Worlds

Ideally, we want to work in Camelot. High on both operational and soulful excellence, these organizations have two

ROIs: return on investment and return on inspiration. Purpose actually improves operational excellence because a laser-like focus creates economies of scale.

Apple, Google, Starbucks, Whole Foods Market, and GE are all Camelots. Inspired by authentic purpose, these high-performing companies and brands are the most distinctive in their industries. Their leaders are as mythical as King Arthur, and their associates are on a crusade.

Working in Camelot takes bravery. In a 24/7 world of 1-minute managers, someone who is reflective, caring, and mindful of the next century is often seen as "out there." When I first started talking to companies about purpose nearly two decades ago, I was met with blank stares and comments such as "That's a 'nice to have'" or "When we get our basics right, we can revisit purpose." The irony, of course, is that nothing is more basic to getting the business on track than purpose. It is foundational.

Most people have seen only a glimpse of the place we call Camelot. The majority of employees work in other structures. There are plantations that are the bastions of incrementalism, the castles in the sky, lofty companies that have a hard time staying aloft, and the fortresses that are companies and brands built to conquer others at all costs. Let's see where you hang your hat.

Working on the Plantation

This scenario isn't very fun. These organizations lack both purpose and performance, and they serve no ideal other than the continued survival of those to whom its resources are entrusted. Plantation organizations are at best opportunistic, and at worst, exploitive. These companies pursue short-term profits, shortsighted goals, the next deal, and a quick return. Associates collect nothing more than paychecks, customers are disgruntled, and leadership simply doesn't exist.

Castle in the Sky Recruiting Now

This organization is based on a fantasy. Castles in the sky are mission-driven companies with great purposes but few systems, processes, or know-how. They feed our imagination but don't put food on the table. These companies recruit with folklore, but once you're in, it's no fairy tale. Many start-ups begin this way, but many also discover in fairly short order that entrepreneurial spirit can take you only so far. No company can thrive without sufficient business skills. Castle in the sky organizations are not self-sustaining—and without money, all the meaning in the world won't end up meaning a thing.

Gates Open at the Fortress

This place is *serious*. Fortresses are superbly managed but insular companies built for one purpose: maximum efficiency. Governed by competitive positioning rather than unlimited possibility, operational efficiency reigns and performance metrics rule. Fortress employees protect their strongholds like good soldiers. They want to annihilate their competitors and become #1. The problem is, this energy is neither sustainable nor healthy. Focusing your arrows on the fortress next door is a distraction from building Camelot.

What Company Do You Work In?

If it's a plantation, I would do some soul searching—then some job searching. If it's a castle in the sky, you will need to add more skill to your will, rigor to your vigor, and precision to your passion. I have created a half-dozen successful companies throughout my career because I had partners that complemented my skill sets. When I cocreated the popular Atlanta restaurant Horseradish Grill, I found partners who had managed restaurants before. When I cocreated a gourmet to fly an airport concept called Plane Delicious, I partnered with the best-known caterers in Georgia. When I cocreated BOTH—both-usa.com, an online back-of-the-house digital platform—my partner Erik Vonk was the leading pioneer in staffing services.

Chances are that most of you work in a fortress—and that's because the fortress is the preferred structure for Western business. It's shareholder-centric and built to beat the other guy so that it can bring more revenue to the bottom line. And there is nothing wrong with that—unless, of course, you actually want your business to help right something that's wrong in the world. Isn't this something all business professionals want? The answer is why we are witnessing the greatest business movement of all time: companies galloping to Camelot.

Your Motivation: What Drives Your Organization?

All four kinds of organizations have distinct approaches in how they run their companies and what they consider most valuable.

- **The plantation** *survives*. It will often cut corners and people to keep its systems going—and since it is in survival mode, it cuts muscle as well as fat. Because employees lack a reason for being, they often see their work as meaningless. Without meaning, nothing much matters, except for eking out a paycheck.
- **The castle in the sky** *dreams*. And while Steven Spielberg says he "dreams for a living" and Albert Einstein wrote, "Imagination is more important than knowledge," having know-how is just as important as knowing *why*.
- **The fortress** *protects*. Last century's corporations hoarded their assets—and rightly so. Shareholder value

was job #1. But the new stakeholder model is bigger and better. Although shareholders hold shares in a company, stakeholders have a stake in the world.

- **Camelot *matters*.** Brilliance of mind and compassion of heart work in union for Camelot companies and brands. According to former IBM president and chief executive officer Sam Palmisano, "All business today faces a new reality. Businesses now operate in a global environment in which long-term societal concerns—in areas from diversity to equal opportunity, the environment and work force policies—have been raised to the same level of public expectation as accounting practices and financial performance."[2]

Your People: What Do They Call You?

Your associates likely address you with respect, but what they call you might be another name. Their title for you will influence the amount of trust and admiration they have for you and their company.

- **A *boss* runs a plantation.** Plantations are bastions of incrementalism. They are run by bosses who care little about anything but profit and are the silent majority of businesses. Many government agencies fall into this category. For instance, a state's Department of Motor Vehicles is usually parked here.
- **A *guru* runs a castle in the sky.** Castles in the sky are companies with lofty purposes, led by gurus who have their heads in the clouds. Unfortunately, their obsession with story *only* distracts them from running their business, which only causes them to falter and suffer. The poster child here is Krispy Kreme. After becoming the darling of Wall Street, Main Street, and Madison Avenue, the company expanded too fast and revenues cooled.[3]

- **A *general* runs a fortress.** Fortresses are companies run by generals. They are built for combat and operate under the theme of competitiveness. Supply chain and chains of command make it impossible for these companies to have meaning beyond making money. Here *psycho*-six-sigma trumps purpose. And this is where most of corporate America is working today. But operational excellence simply isn't enough anymore.

- **A *hero* runs Camelot.** Like the knights of the Round Table, this leadership is brave, purposeful, and noble. Heroes do what is good, not just what is right. They are in search of what King Arthur called the Holy Grail. Apple's Steve Jobs, Google's Eric Schmidt, GE's Jeffrey Immelt, and IBM's Sam Palmisano are all examples of well-known—and highly regarded—Camelot leaders. And these leaders don't just run corporations. The term *Camelot* is often used to refer admiringly to the presidency of John F. Kennedy, a man whose term many proclaimed had the greatest potential and promise for the future.

Your Employees

How do employees in these different kinds of companies work?

- **People who work on plantations are the *hardest working*.** The problem is, without purpose, they don't know what they are working *for*. Because plantations work like machines, their employees can feel like cogs in a wheel. And also like a machine, the whole system goes down when one part is missing or breaks. These people work for money, not for meaning.

- **People employed by a castle in the sky have their heads in the clouds.** These dreamers imagine—and often create—a better world. These are mission-critical people; however, they're often on a mission without a vision. They are great teammates but not necessarily great team players.

- **On the other end of this spectrum, fortress associates are guarded.** They don't let their hair down. They're usually dogmatic and autocratic, and they let people know that it's their way or the highway. They guard their posts (jobs) like watchdogs. And they will protect their fiefdom even if it means defeating another associate. Fortress associates are often doubtful, skeptical, and perhaps worst of all, cynical and judgmental of others' ideas—because if they don't win the day themselves, it could mean a proverbial beheading tomorrow.

- **However, Camelot is different from all of these. Because you don't work at Camelot; you are *called* there.** Authentic and genuine individuals are doing business in Camelot every day. They support one another's ideas and celebrate one another's successes. They make decisions that are focused, not fearful. And they keep their eyes on the next quarter as well as the next quarter century.

Decisions: How Are They Made?

- **Behind closed doors (plantations):** Because plantations work without purpose, they usually work without collaboration as well. When only a handful of leaders are making decisions, it frequently leads to something called *groupthink*, a psychological phenomenon that occurs when a group of people who desire harmony override a realistic appraisal of alternatives and viewpoints. Welcome to Enron, where top executives locked themselves in their corporate tower and convinced one another that they were about to do a noble thing.

- **On the mountaintop (castles in the sky):** Culture suffers in leader-centered versus group-centered organizations. Castle in the sky leaders are high and mighty, but when their people say they would fall off a cliff for a leader, they usually will. Communication giant WorldCom might have appeared to be the next coming, but its billions in earnings was an illusion. They had to come down from the mountain to file the largest bankruptcy in United States history.

- **From the pulpit (fortresses):** Sermons are for Saturdays and Sundays, not workdays. Fortress leaders tend to elevate and promote themselves beyond the title of chief executive officer (CEO) to deity-like figures. They espouse the gospel of business according to them. *Know-it-alls* are better served by having the *wherewithal* to listen first with their hearts before delivering headstrong oratory. That's how leaders do it in Camelot.

- **Around the Round Table (Camelot):** Nothing is more gratifying than being part of a decision in business. In Camelot companies, *team rules*. In a minor but masterful move, IBM's Palmisano changed the name of his leadership group to a leadership "team," thereby sending the message throughout the organization that winning was a team sport. Whole Foods Market did something similar by creating *its* Whole Foods Declaration of Interdependence that gives clear direction to all its stakeholders that they must work as an ecosystem to be truly successful.[4] Depending on one another is the ultimate team sport.

Thinking: What's the Prevailing Mind-set?

- **Computer thinking (plantations):** Plantation companies are run by technology. "The computer won't let me make that change" is often the excuse heard here. Whether it's a car rental reservation or tallying products, computer-driven transactions delete compassion. It's time to give people the power to override technology.

- **Out-of-the-box thinking (castles in the sky):** Unencumbered by making profits, we can become prophets.

  Granted Muhammad, Buddha, Jesus Christ, and Moses were not businesspeople, but their visions inspired the biggest brands of all—religions. People who are on a mission usually ascend to the top of their industries, such as Apple's Steve Jobs and Southwest Airlines' Herb Kelleher, not to mention the man who imagined the most beautiful world of all: singer and composer John Lennon.

- **In-the-box thinking (fortresses):** Routinization drives out innovation in fortress companies. If you are being held captive inside a fortress, you are going to have to break out if you want a breakthrough.

- **Breakthrough thinking (Camelot):** Albert Einstein was fond of what he called combinatorial play. This is when both sides of the brain play together. "Creativity is intelligence having fun," he wrote.

  Creative minds welcome questions, puzzles, mysteries, and problems. There are no obstacles. Camelot itself is a mind-set. As lyricist Alan Jay Lerner described it, "It's true! It's true! The crown has made it clear. The climate must be perfect all the year."[5]

Look: How Do They View the World of Business?

- **Closed-eyed (plantations):** Plantations are known for their insularity. These companies have a narrow view of business and are satisfied with making the quota. At the end of the day it's about just that: the end of the day.

- **Wide-eyed (castles in the sky):** Although scoffed at by cynics, skeptics, and doubters, castle in the sky leaders view business as a way to make their dreams come true.

- **Steely-eyed (fortresses):** Jack Welch was the epitome of last century's tough, steely-eyed autocratic fortress leader. He saw business as a battlefield. But Neutron Jack, as they called him, has been disarmingly frank in retrospect: "On the face of it shareholder value is the dumbest idea in the world," quipped the former GE CEO.[6]

- **Open-eyed (Camelot):** Camelot companies view business as part of a bigger system—one for which they are responsible. Purposeful Camelot companies want to be best *for* the world, not just in the world. They practice what I call *optimal diversity*, that is, recognizing that every decision the organization makes affects all life-forms within our ecosystem.

Advantage: What Is the Organization's Edge in the Marketplace?

- **Reactive (plantations):** Plantations do whatever the market tells them to do. Without greater purpose, these organizations often become the price leader whose only goal is to offer more for less. As a result, they develop ricochet cultures that can't sustain rocky times.

  With the inability to move products because they were unable to move into the future, an electronics giant laid off their highest-paid employees and replaced them with cheaper workers. This was done while their CEO got a $7 million paycheck. It didn't add up. Goodbye, Circuit City.[7]

- **Differentiated (castles in the sky):** "Think different" is how Apple's Steve Jobs started out. While all the computer companies at the time were focusing on putting more power into their machines, Jobs wanted to put more power into people's hands. His fledgling castle in the sky was taken over by John Scully in 1985, but Jobs would return in hero's journey fashion in 1995 and make Apple his and our beloved Camelot.

- **Competitive (fortresses):** Fortress companies are in a fight to the death. These bulwarks of defense are always up for a fight. And watch out. They want to win at any price. Usually the costs include cutbacks in time off and people. With the loss of greater purpose comes a lesser company. Competitive advantage is an oxymoron here, because in today's market, defensiveness is not enough.

- **Distinctive (Camelot):** What makes America such a distinctive brand is our values. David Gergen, White House author of the insightful book *Eyewitness to Power*, states, "A President's central purpose must be rooted in the nation's core values. They can be found in the Declaration of Independence. Lincoln said he never had a political sentiment that did not spring from it. It is our communal vision."[8] Camelot brands grown from their distinctive origins create *one and only* cultures. Hence, they are indispensable in the marketplace.

Their Constituents

Who are these companies developed for—and what is the result? (See Figure 13.2.)

- **Plantations are built for the owners.** Companies and brands built for owners set us back a hundred years when we were branding cattle to guarantee our neighbors knew "that's mine."

- **Castles in the sky are created for employees and customers.** The best cultures start in high places. With lofty ideas but without operational expertise, your company will not get off the ground. Even if you have the next big idea, unless it happens, it's worthless.
- **Fortresses are constructed for shareholders.** These monolithic corporations have one goal: amass as much wealth as possible for the kings of Wall Street—shareholders. Ask anything more of them, and they close the gates.
- **Camelots rise for all—not just shareholders, but each and every stakeholder.** "The larger the company, the greater its moral imperative to take responsibility for its multi-faceted impact on the world," writes Jag Sheth, author of *Firms of Endearment*.[9]

	PLANTATION	CASTLE	FORTRESS	CAMELOT
YOUR TITLE	Boss	Guru	General	Hero
YOUR MOTIVATION	To Survive	To Dream	To Protect	To Matter
YOUR EMPLOYEES	Ambivalent	Head in the Clouds	Guarded	Authentic
YOUR DECISIONS	Behind Closed Doors	On a Mountaintop	From a Pulpit	Around a Round Table
YOUR THINKING	Computer	Out of the Box	In the Box	Curious
YOUR LOOK	Closed	Wide-Eyed	Steely-Eyed	Open-Eyed
YOUR ADVANTAGE	Reactive	Differentiated	Competitive	Distinctive
YOUR DRIVERS	Growth and Acquisition	Ideals	Processes	Alignment
YOUR CONSTITUENTS	Founders and Management	Employees and Customers	Shareholders	All

FIGURE 13.2   Camelot Matrix, Detail

Source: © BrightHouse. Illustration by David Paprocki.

Questions for the Quest

BrightHouse clients who strive to be Camelots often want to know where they are on the journey. To determine where your brands stand, start with these questions. To help you pinpoint your location, use your organization to answer these questions.

1. Do you understand the founding sentiments that made your organization thrive in the first place?
2. Can you articulate meaningful organizational values shared and lived by all (without checking your employee handbook)?
3. Do you feel inspired to go to work each day?
4. Does your organization leave the communities in which it interacts better off than it found them?
5. Do you create something more significant than products and services?
6. Is your company's leader one of your heroes?
7. Do you earn profits in a way that is consistent with your purpose, and does working toward that purpose enable you to earn profits?
8. Does your organization fully embrace its commitment to the stand it takes?
9. Do people care more about doing the job right than about just getting it done?
10. Is your company engaged in a process of continuous learning?
11. Is your organization on a trajectory to be better tomorrow than it is today?

Answering the Call

To locate your brand, place it in the center of the grid shown in Figure 13.3. First move vertically, then diagonally, and then horizontally. The size of each move should be based on the degree to which you feel strongly about your response to the preceding questions. For most questions, you will probably want to move only a space, but if you feel strongly about the answer to a question, move two, or even three spaces.

Questions 1 to 4 are the fundamental components of a Master Idea. Move up for each "yes" answer and down for each "no."

Questions 5 through 8 are more complex. They measure the alignment between the Master Idea and its execution. They ask if the company not only strives toward a distinctive, authentic, and significant purpose but also succeeds in doing so in an effective, inspirational, and stakeholder-responsive way. Move northeast for each affirmative response and southwest for each negative one.

Questions 9 to 11 measure excellence in execution. Although we have shown that it is an unsustainable position, many organizations are extremely effective in the short run, even in the absence of an overarching higher purpose. For each of these questions, a positive response moves you to the right; a negative one moves you to the left.

These questions are designed very broadly to serve as a platform for raising specific queries that relate directly to your organization and industry. This is the imperfect start to the beginning of a deep examination. The objective is to frame your business in a new brighter light.

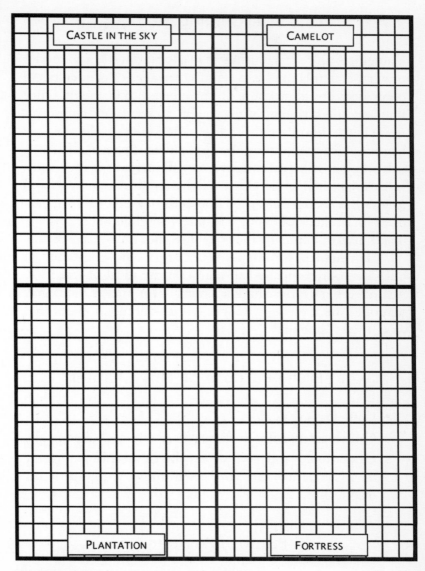

FIGURE 13.3 Camelot Square Workbook

Source: © BrightHouse. Illustration by David Paprocki.

One Brief Shining Moment

Camelot is more of a journey than a location. It is a reminder of what business can be, do, and say in service of society. All companies are somewhere on the journey to Camelot. Once they're called, organizations begin to reinvent themselves to be better brands and brighter companies. And once they begin to take the journey, the companies are never the same. Advocacy, alignment, and revenues all increase dramatically.

Amazon CEO Jeff Bezos tells his employees to *work hard, have fun, and make history*.[10] Thousands of employees are on a mission. Millions of happy customers and billions in revenue makes Bezos's company the congenial spot called Camelot.

Through passion, sharing of story, and constancy of purpose your company can maintain the ideal of Camelot. Again Lerner's lyrics share a lesson, "Don't let it be forgot, that once there was a spot for one brief shining moment that was called Camelot."[11]

What Is the Purpose of This Chapter?

- Camelot is real.
- Camelot companies are distinctive, therefore indispensable.
- Operational and soulful excellence combined result in ROI: return on your investment and return on inspiration.

Purpose Pointers

- Take the Camelot test in this chapter.
- People don't work at Camelot; they are called there.
- Who will you take on your journey to Camelot?

14

A World on Purpose

Purpose is a force as strong as gravity, but instead of pulling things down, it pushes them forward.

—Joey Reiman,
on the science of purpose

She was only 17 years old when she was invited to the Apollo Theatre in Harlem to dance before a sellout crowd. Poised and polished from years of performance, this young woman said a prayer and stepped onto the stage. With intimidation from the previous dancers, Ella shocked the crowd and decided to sing.

Ella Fitzgerald brings the house down, wins $25, and changes the world of song forever.[1] This is the story of purpose. When Fitzgerald recognized her true talent in life, she was living her purpose. It wasn't what she had originally signed up to do. But it was what she knew she *had* to do.

Fifty years ago, John Fitzgerald Kennedy challenged our nation to put a man on the moon. In doing so, he recalled America's ethos of forging the next frontier. For those settlers, the direction was west. For President Kennedy, it was north—to the stars.

The president visited NASA. During his tour, he met a janitor. The president asked, "Sir, what do you do here?" The janitor replied, "Mr. President, I'm helping to put a man on the moon." He might have been sweeping the floor, but he was part of something as big as the moon.

These are true stories of purpose. Whether you are the president of the United States or a janitor, purpose lifts and liberates everyone. Imagine your company filled with Ella Fitzgeralds or run by John Fitzgerald Kennedy. Do you know anyone at work as proud as that janitor? Are you part of a crew that is about to accomplish something never done before?

If we are to live and work in a world on purpose, we have to ask ourselves: "What is *my* purpose?"

This simple exercise just might help you find out:

I have been teaching the concept of purpose at Emory University's Goizueta School of Business for more than a decade. Every semester, I ask a classroom full of BBAs and MBAs what they hope to do when they graduate. As you would imagine, the answers range from working in investment banking to getting a gig at a high-powered consultancy firm such as the Boston Consulting Group. I list all their aspirations on the blackboard.

Then I write each of them a check from the Bank of Dreams for $25 million. Asking them to suspend any suspicion that the money is not real, I pull another blackboard down over the first one and ask them for their dreams.

Those same business students now come up with entirely different answers. They range from becoming a professional golfer, to opening a school in Sri Lanka, to creating a rehab center in Hawaii that helps addicts recover by teaching them how to surf.

Unencumbered by the aspirations of high net worth—a bar set by their parents, peers, and many business professors—they talk of their real dreams for a better world in service to those here now and generations to come.

I ask the class of 70 students to pull out their cell phones and take a picture of their dreams. This is their snapshot of a world on purpose. At the end of class, I pull the first board of aspirations over the second of dreams and remind them that whatever they do with their lives, the board behind this one should drive the one in front of it—just like a company's Master Idea should drive the business.

In this new era for business and marketing, the best brands will be built *on purpose*—on a fundamental human truth, a universal good, a deep-seated conviction that outlasts campaigns, opens minds, deepens relationships, and grows share, of both profits and people.

The Industrial Revolution was built with our hands and the Technology Revolution with our heads. The next movement, the Human Revolution, will be forged with our hearts. This shift will require us to engage our spirits, liberate our creativity, and unleash our personal passion.

Because each of us is here on purpose, we already have what it takes. Now we need to take it to work and work on purpose. This book is only a toolbox. You are the builder. As dear friend and president of Newell Rubbermaid Professional Group Bill Burke wrote to me in a letter—now framed in the Aristotle conference room at BrightHouse, "Think deeply, act soulfully and win meaningfully." When you do that, you are guaranteed a lasting legacy.

A Modern-Day Fairy Tale for Business

Roz Chast's "Story Template" cartoon (from the Introduction) is a great way to think about our story as well. Business was a great idea, but the wheels came off the tracks. Fortunately, purpose got business back on track, and now when my son Alden tells me he wants to go into business, I smile because there is no better place to change the world.

Once Upon a Time

Way back in the nineteenth century there was this big idea called *business* that transformed a land of farmers and small shops into an Industrial Revolution. Men got rich, driven by the locomotive of power. Three of these men—J. P. Morgan, Andrew Carnegie, and John D. Rockefeller—wanted to be the richest, which they accomplished with another big idea called *capitalism*.

But unlike another idea called *democracy*, which is based on equality, capitalism banked on *in*equality. In essence, the bigger you were, the better you were. But wait . . . what about famed economist Adam Smith's essay published in 1776 titled *Wealth of Nations?* After all, it wasn't called wealth of individuals. In a nutshell, Smith argued that the benefits of the free market should go to *society* and that the average man and woman should be the primary beneficiaries of a wealthy nation.

The US government had the answer and provided it in 1913. The Federal Reserve Act established a central bank that would supervise monetary policy, taking the nation's money supply out of the money moguls' pockets.[2] Wow, now *everyone*—not just business barons—could get rich. As President Calvin Coolidge declared in the 1920s, "After all, the chief business of the American people is business."[3]

Suddenly

But not so fast, Calvin. In 1929, the Great Depression put 13 million people out of work, and President Franklin Roosevelt said, "The measure of restoration lies in the extent we apply social values and purpose more nobly than mere profit." When he left office, our nation was in pretty good shape—except, of course, for the world war that was being waged between some of the world's most powerful nations.[4]

Over the next 50 years, capitalism gave way to yet another big idea called *corporate America*. In this world, business makes money for shareholders, even at the expense of human and natural resources. Of course, we paid a price for this. Many of the structures on which we depended, such as social security and the gold watch, have all but disappeared. By 2008, people were out of work, out of pocket, and going out of their minds. World economies faced bankruptcy, *Homo sapiens* had become *Homo consumens* looking for happiness in things, and life was on "orange alert." As for the environment, we couldn't throw things out because there is no "out" anymore. And this brings us to today.

Luckily

Business discovered the biggest idea of all: purpose. One brand after another recognized that meaning matters to their people—and that business can be the lead character in improving the story of humanity. Business enterprise redefines another idea called progress. It's not just about getting ahead but about having a heart. Business and its leadership want to save the world.

Although many great business leaders, such as IBM's Thomas Watson, Hershey's Milton Hershey, and Nestlé's Henri Nestlé, had led with a sense of purpose in the past, this era would be the first time in history that business expanded its orbit of caring beyond shareholders—to the world at large.

Happily Ever After

Business leaders will lead their armies to battle not one another, as they have previously, but to battle instead the ills of the world. Marketers will bring meaning to their goods and services. Human resources will become resources for humans. Strategy will move from a plan to make another lose to a process through which *everyone wins*. And instead of becoming whatever the marketplace wants us to be, we will seek the instructive fire that we can all find in our own beginnings.

As we've learned from purpose-led companies and brands, business can create a positive presence in the world. By being the hero in the larger story of life, business can revitalize the sectors of health, education, equality, and sustainability.

Which Goliath Will *Your* Company Slay?

In September 2000, 189 world leaders came together at the United Nations Headquarters in New York to adopt the United Nations Millennium Declaration.[5] This document committed the involved nations to a new global partnership to reduce and mitigate the ills of the world. The Millennium Development Goals (MDGs) are[6]:

1. Eradicate extreme poverty and hunger
2. Achieve universal primary education
3. Promote gender equality and empower women
4. Reduce child mortality
5. Improve maternal health
6. Combat HIV/AIDS, malaria, and other diseases
7. Ensure environmental sustainability
8. Develop a global partnership for development

Which one of these Goliaths resonates most with your company and purpose? Which one compels you to aim your business or brand towards?

We can slay these and other Goliaths by being champions of diversity, benefactors of the arts, protectors of the environment, advocates of human and civil rights, promoters of personal and public health, providers for the impoverished and hungry, supporters of self-esteem and self-worth, defenders of animal rights and protection—whatever cause our unique purpose enables us to uniquely support.

How to Make a Dent in the Universe

The MDGs not only demanded social change but gave it a deadline: 2015. And although we certainly won't be able to right all the world's wrongs within the next few years, business can make what Steve Jobs called a "dent in the universe"— and make at least the very first purposeful steps toward this.

Procter & Gamble (P&G), for instance, saw the MDGs as motivation to do more. It used the opportunities that the MDGs presented and built on the strengths already inherent in P&G's ethos of improving lives every day. In 2004, P&G refined its Pur water purification systems, making global strides. For its efforts, P&G was recognized with the international ICC/UNDP World Business Award in support of the MDGs. P&G continues to use its unique talents to catalyze social impact authentically and with fervor, while reaching ever forward.[7]

Nestlé has also made the MDGs its mission. Building on its foundational character, its ethos of good food for a good life, it has cultivated sustainable development through dozens of programs in more than 30 countries—initiatives that range from supporting dairy farmers to furthering coffee development in China. Aligned with its goals, a growing Nestlé is helping the world grow. For cultivating this global growth and to recognize Nestlé's coffee development programs in China, the company was awarded the 2012 World Business Award.[8]

In 2010, a United Nations summit was held for three days to review the goals once more. This meeting resulted in the pledge of more than $40 billion in resources from "governments, the private sector, foundations, international organizations, civil society, and research organizations" in order to further women's and children's health.[9]

Coming Together on Purpose

Companies and nations have together made huge strides in the areas of alleviating extreme poverty, decreasing child mortality, and increasing access to water. However, the Millennium Development Goal of reducing the number of people without access to basic sanitation is lagging behind. Plenty more Goliaths exist out there, including gender inequality, hunger, and the prevalence of urban slums.

The good news is that there are companies and company leaders working to change this every day. According to American Standard chief executive officer (CEO) Jay Gould, "Sanitation is the most vital prerequisite for health and quality of life. Without sanitation systems that work, disease proliferates, dignity suffers, death tolls rise." And yet, 2.5 billion people remain without sufficient sanitation facilities. Who better to "raise the standard" (American Standard's Master Idea) in every corner of the world than American Standard?

Jay continues, "We know from our work with the Gates Foundation, data available from the CDC (Centers for Disease Control and Prevention) and our own research that over 2,000 children are dying every day as a result of diarrheal diseases." American Standard can and will make a difference by providing a platform for American consumers to join a brand that's willing to take a stand.

The United Nations continues to charge forward toward a common purpose; fortunately, they are not alone. Organizations like the World Health Organization and UNICEF are working with businesses such as Banco Itaú, the largest private bank in the southern hemisphere, to support the MDGs (according to a December 31, 2011, report by Bloomberg), as well as other organizations that have taken their own routes to answer the call to global action.

Marketer as Healer

I was first introduced to this inspiring term by way of my dear colleague Jag Sheth's book *Firms of Endearment* in 2007. Since then I have thought about how I might put it into practice: our nation will spend $350 billion this year to market more than 150,000 products to 300 million ailing Americans. Obesity, heart disease, and our sedentary century have put us on the doctor's rounds.

The growing movement toward anticonsumerism and more purpose-filled marketing has created another fruitful intersection for marketing's new role in a world of need. It might not be a total cure; however, it is a step toward helping America get healthy again—and it elevates the role of the marketing industry in the process.

Here is an idea that moves business from seller to healer. The Alliance to Make US Healthiest is a grassroots effort to help make the United States one of the healthiest nations again. BrightHouse offered up the idea of the 1/10 of 1 percent marketing credit to make marketers caregivers as well. This is how it works: The marketing industry spends $250 billion a year. If we put aside 1/10 of 1 percent, $250 million could be spent to help heal America by supporting programs like the Alliance to Make US Healthiest.[10]

The Unified Theory of Purpose

The Story of Purpose began in the beginning. With the big bang came a purposive force that has never stopped—and, according to physicists, that never will. The continually expansive universe gave birth to the stars, the planets, and you and me. As we are contributions of this purpose, it's no wonder that our own bodies have a cellular purpose of their own: to grow and create unions with one another.

"Purpose is in every particle and every cell, compound, mass and form of energy in the cosmos. The anthropic principle has even raised the serious consideration that the universe itself has a purpose," wrote Emory University professor Corey Keyes.[11]

Is purpose, then, a framework we human beings created to make meaning? Or is purpose simply an inherent part of our existence, like gravity? If the former is the case—and purpose is human-made—then it represents a hypothetical construct. This means there will be doubt about it, because humans constructed the model. However, if purpose is innate—if it exists because it always has—it is an intervening variable that no one needs to prove.

Hypothetical structures are human-made and therefore can be *un*made. This is not true, however, when something is innate. Here, the force is revealed. And we recognize it as implicit. So, what do you think? Is purpose a construct for finding meaning or an inherent power like gravity? For deeper understanding of the elemental power of purpose and its unifying nature, we look to nature herself.

The Best Business Model on Earth

If you want to see how a perfect business is run, throw out everything you learned in business school and look outside the window. The Earth has been in business for 3.8 billion years based on a highly sustainable, scalable model and fairly simple purpose: to support life.

But humankind attempted to subdue Earth. In less than 100 years, we undid billions of years of careful balance by trying to reengineer the way nature works. We did the same with business. What started out as an idea to support life became a life-threatening game.

The Earth has set an example for organizations. She's built distinctive species that work interdependently. What if we applied that lens to our companies and brands? What if the products and services we sold encouraged us to work *better* together?

Like nature, union is living and procreative. It's a new (old) and different construct where buyer and seller are responsible; two parts become intimate and bond into one greater than its parts.

Purpose is not limited to a single goal such as winning but is rather aimed toward energizing all in its path. Whether we called them natural resources or human resources, we have acted as if they were there for the taking. And we took them.

Once we understand we are part of something bigger, we see that nature, and our planet, are full of lessons for doing business in a profitable and sustainable manner. The idea is the basis for a movement called biomimicry, from the Greek *bios*, meaning "life,"[12] and *mimesis*, meaning "imitation."[13] This movement promises a blend of Earth and worth. Nature can serve as a model, a measure, and a mentor for business, says biologist Janine Benyus, one of the movement's leaders and author of *Biomimicry: Innovation Inspired by Nature*.

In her book, she summarizes the idea of biomimicry as a solution-seeking tool. She goes on to discuss the wide range of problems or design challenges one might be trying to solve and how we should ask ourselves how nature would do this, as nature has been doing this for millions of years and has probably figured it out.

The Purpose Reset

Why has business taken so long to recognize and harness the power of purpose? Perhaps we got the idea of business wrong in the first place. It was not to transact but to transform. The world is hungry for food, safety, and meaning. Business has the power to reset the whole place in which we live. The bottom line is *unity*—and purpose unifies everything. Business is the messenger that can deliver the message.

The *why* behind purpose is the concept of union. Religious wars, partisan politics, economic divides, and the battle between meaning and money are breaking us up into haves and have-nots. But once we adopt purpose, we will set the limits of unbridled expansion of centralized authority.

Coming apart will break us. Coming together will make us. And we can come together through a new era in business.

Business has come to a fork in the road. One path is exploitive: people compete with one another and deplete themselves on behalf of profit. This exploitation leads to dehumanization and eventually annihilation. Think about it. The only time a competitor is happy is when only he or she remains.

The other path, unworn and beckoning, is purposeful. People use profits to optimize their own and others' lives. This humanization leads us to a collective quality called union where the world is truly one.

It's our choice. The world is left with one business standing or the world whole and prospering. Your story of purpose will help determine the outcome.

What Is the Purpose of This Chapter?

- The best companies and brands are built on purpose—on a fundamental human truth, a universal good, a deep-seated conviction that opens minds, deepens relationships, outlasts campaigns, and grows both profits and people.
- Purpose is a great force that has been present since the dawn of time. It is our responsibility as businesspeople to harness it to engage our spirits, liberate our creativity, and unleash our personal passion and compassion for others.
- Fierce competition is not sustainable. Compassion is. In the decades to come, business will focus on the business of life and will work for the largest client of all—humanity.

Purpose Pointers

- Purpose is unifying.
- Purpose is a force of nature and is here to stay.
- If you put humanity back in business, business will come back for good.

Epilogue

Collective Purpose Is Our Saving Grace

The happiest ending is also a new beginning.

—Joey Reiman,
on the future of business

Imagine the world the way it ought to be. Like its predecessor, the universe, it would be ever expanding and ever contributing. Life would be fuller, people would be happier, and our planet would flourish. Our civilization would have reached a higher purpose together by serving our world.

Instead, we have reached a boiling point. Terror, a failing economy, a climate in trouble, and a crisis in meaning have created a world that is burning. So what question does humanity ask now that the world is burning?

It's the same question people have asked since we could grunt: "Why?"

If we could start over, this is where we would begin—by asking why, or "For what purpose?" In a sense, the mere act of asking provides the answer, because the question of why then becomes the quest for *how*.

This is not a book with an end, but one that prompts a beginning. A lot of authors write books about lots of subjects. Many try to bring their text to a definitive close. This book departs from that model; my intent is not to make a

209

terminal point but to generate a variety of extensions and applications for work on purpose.

This is how.

When we live and work on purpose, we have the ability to positively affect society and all the systems that support it: health, commerce, and governance. Health on purpose enables humanity to live better. Commerce on purpose gives rise to fruitful work. And governance on purpose rights the laws for mutualized benefit.

Collectively, these domains on purpose create the presence of positive in the world. In an Olympian sense, collective purpose is our saving grace.

Marching Forward

The Story of Purpose is a book about marching forward. Without purpose, we have no direction. With purpose we have our marching orders.

Purpose drives everything we do. It turns asking into acting, an idea into an "I did it," and a job into a calling. Purpose is emotion in motion, faith in fifth gear, and a reason to charge into work in the morning. Once you find it, no force is greater.

Since we humans are creatures that seek meaning, most people know they *need* purpose. But the fact is that companies need purpose, too. And the ones that have found a larger purpose than profit have become the most profitable organizations on Earth—because they work in the company of something greater.

That's why I created a day called March Fourth, a day on which you *march forth* on your purpose, to something bigger.

Declaring your purpose is no small feat. Sometimes it takes an act of Congress.

On March 4, 1789, the US Constitution went into effect. It also used to be the day that the president of the United States was sworn into office.[1]

The first year I opened my office, I gave people time off on March Fourth. It wasn't really about taking a day off as much as taking the day *on*. Some of my colleagues went to work and created new ideas that rocked their worlds. Other colleagues went skydiving or to cooking schools. One signed up to build a hospital in Guatemala, another got engaged, and yet another made a life-saving decision. What they all had in common was that they chose to move toward living a more purposeful life on that day.

The date March 4 also played an important role in the writing of this book, because it was on that date in 1957 that the S&P 500 stock market index was introduced—and the story of purpose began.

This index is considered the bellwether for the American economy. Today, business uses the S&P 500 as a measuring stick for financial success. But as you learned from this book, there is a new measure in town: purpose. Purpose-driven companies outperform S&P 500 companies by as much as 1,025 percent.[2]

That's why purpose is a story business can't put down. And it's why the world's best companies are marching forward. Every business has a story. What's yours?

Notes

Introduction

1. http://www.ted.com/talks/brene_brown_on_vulnerability.html.
2. Corey Keyes, "Authentic Purpose: The Spiritual Infrastructure of Life," *Journal of Management, Spirituality & Religion: An International Refereed Journal 8 (December 2011)*. Reprinted by permission of Taylor & Francis, LTD.

Chapter 1 The Purpose of Work Is to Work on Purpose

1. http://money.cnn.com/magazines/fortune/fortune500_archive/full/1955/index.html.
2. http://www.nytimes.com/2011/09/04/opinion/sunday/do-happier-people-work-harder.html.
3. Latin etymology of *vocation*, http://www.etymonline.com/index.php?allowed_in_frame=0&search=vocation&searchmode=none.
4. Adapted from Brian Selznick, *The Invention of Hugo Cabret* (New York: Scholastic Inc./Scholastic Press, 2007). Copyright © 2007 by Brian Selznick. Used by permission.

Chapter 2 Purpose-Inspired Leadership

1. Latin meaning of *motive*, http://www.etymonline.com/index.php?allowed_in_frame=0&search=motive&searchmode=none.
2. Albert Einstein, *Albert Einstein, The Human Side*, ed. Helen Dukas and Banesh Hoffmann (Princeton, NJ: Princeton University Press, 1979). © 1979 By the Estate of Albert Einstein, Princeton

University Press. Reprinted by permission of Princeton University Press.

3. Yvon Chouinard, *Let My People Go Surfing: The Education of a Reluctant Businessman* (New York: Penguin Publishing, 2005), 178.

4. Herman Hesse, *The Journey to the East* (New York: Martino Fine Books, 2011), 25.

5. http://www.nytimes.com/1999/10/04/business/akio-morita-co-founder-of-sony-and-japanese-business-leader-dies-at-78 .html?pagewanted=all&src=pm.

6. http://athome.harvard.edu/programs/nagy/threads/concept_of_hero.html.

7. Latin etymology of *amicus curiae*, http://www.etymonline.com /index.php?allowed_in_frame=0&search=friend+of+the+court &searchmode=nl.

8. http://online.wsj.com/article/SB1000142405274870386420457 6315223305697158.html.

Chapter 3   The Master Idea

1. Theodore Roszak, *The Cult of Information: A Neo-Luddite Treatise on High Tech, Artificial Intelligence, and the True Art of Thinking*, 3rd ed. (Berkeley: University of California Press, 1994). Reproduced with permission of University of California Press via Copyright Clearance Center, Inc.

2. Theodore Roszak (Professor of history at California State University, East Bay), interview by Joey Reiman, Berkeley, CA, May 1998.

3. http://www.forbes.com/sites/marketshare/2012/02/16/the-most-valuable-company-in-the-world/.

4. http://investor.google.com/corporate/code-of-conduct.html.

5. http://www.starbucks.com/blog/what-s-your-starbucks-signature/674.

6. Blake Mycoskie, *Start Something That Matters* (New York: Spiegel & Grau, 2011).

7. http://www.youtube.com/watch?v=Rco9xujjAak; also was an advertisement as seen here: http://www.youtube.com/watch?v=ImE8ZyoKUaQ&feature=fvwrel.

8. http://www.nike.com.

9. http://www.guardian.co.uk/business/2012/jan/08/virgin-brands-richard-branson-owns; http://www.virgin.com/company.
10. http://www-03.ibm.com/ibm/history/multimedia/fulldescriptions/think.html.
11. Latin origin of *spirit*, http://www.etymonline.com/index.php?allowed_in_frame=0&search=spiritus&searchmode=nl.
12. http://www.wholefoodsmarket.com/company/history.php.
13. http://thewaltdisneycompany.com/about-disney/company-overview; www.disneyinternational.com.
14. http://www.unilever.com/mediacentre/newsandfeatures/keithweednamedmarketeroftheyear.aspx.
15. "Others." Permission via Bob Watson.
16. Roszak, *The Cult of Information*.

Chapter 4 Ethos

1. Greek origin of *etymology*, http://www.etymonline.com/index.php?allowed_in_frame=0&search=etymology&searchmode=none.
2. Latin origin of *corporation*, http://www.etymonline.com/index.php?term=corporation&allowed_in_frame=0.
3. Latin origin of *history*, http://www.etymonline.com/index.php?term=story&allowed_in_frame=0.

Chapter 5 Culture

1. http://www.walkawayusa.com/.
2. Greek origin of *symbolon*, http://www.etymonline.com/index.php?term=symbol&allowed_in_frame=0.
3. http://www.everythingpanam.com/1946_-_1960.html.
4. http://www.southwest.com/html/about-southwest/index.html.
5. Latin origin of *religion*, http://www.etymonline.com/index.php?term=religion&allowed_in_frame=0.
6. Ben Cohen and Jerry Greenfield, *Ben and Jerry's Double-Dip: How to Run a Values-Led Business and Make Money, Too* (New York: Simon & Schuster, 1997). Reprinted with permission of

Simon & Schuster, Inc. Copyright © 1997 by Ben Cohen and Jerry Greenfield.

7. Cohen and Greenfield, *Ben and Jerry's Double-Dip.*
8. http://www.hersheystory.org/about/milton-hershey.aspx.
9. Greek origin of *respect*, http://www.etymonline.com/index.php?term=respect&allowed_in_frame=0.

Chapter 6   Values

1. http://about.zappos.com/our-unique-culture/zappos-core-values/deliver-wow-through-service.

Chapter 7   Strategy

1. Greek origin of *strategy*, http://www.etymonline.com/index.php?term=strategy&allowed_in_frame=0.
2. http://www.cemex.com/SustainableDevelopment/High ImpactSocialPrograms.aspx.
3. Stuart L. Hart, *Capitalism at the Crossroads: Aligning Business, Earth, and Humanity*, 2nd ed. (Upper Saddle River, NJ: Pearson Education, 2008). © 2008. Reprinted by permission of Pearson Education, Inc., Upper Saddle River, NJ.
4. Latin origin of *competition*, http://www.etymonline.com/index.php?term=competition&allowed_in_frame=0.
5. http://www.history.com/this-day-in-history/three-point-seatbelt-inventor-nils-bohlin-born.

Chapter 8   Tactics

1. Latin origin of *communication*, http://www.etymonline.com/index.php?term=communication&allowed_in_frame=0.
2. http://www.businessinsider.com/starbucks-is-giving-out-free-coffee-this-fourth-of-july-2012-7.
3. http://www.nike.com.

4. http://www.itworld.com/internet/127141/google-give-all-employees-10-raise-1000-cash-bonus.
5. Robert Spector and Patrick D. McCarthy, *The Nordstrom Way: The Inside Story of America's #1 Customer Service Company*, 2nd ed. (New York: John Wiley & Sons Inc., 2000), 34. Reprinted with permission of John Wiley and Sons, Inc.
6. http://solutions.3m.com/wps/portal/3M/en_US/3M-Company/Information/AboutUs/.
7. http://www.walmartstores.com/sites/sustainabilityreport/2007/associatesPersonal.html.
8. http://www.forbes.com/2009/02/12/layoffs-workforce-planning-leadership-management_0212_kneale.html.
9. http://cobweb2.louisville.edu/faculty/regbruce/bruce//cases/harley/harley.htm.
10. Rajendra S. Sisodia, David B. Wolfe, and Jagdish N. Sheth, *Firms of Endearment: How World-Class Companies Profit from Passion and Purpose*, 1st ed. (Upper Saddle River, NJ: Pearson Education, 2007). © 2007. Reprinted by permission of Pearson Education, Inc., Upper Saddle River, NJ.
11. Old English origin of *brand*, http://www.etymonline.com/index.php?term=brand&allowed_in_frame=0.
12. http://www.coneinc.com/content1090.
13. http://investor.google.com/corporate/code-of-conduct.html.
14. http://www.stefan-gassner.de/dokumente/starbucks.pdf.
15. Greek origin of *philanthropy*, http://www.etymonline.com/index.php?term=philanthropy&allowed_in_frame=0.

Part III   Purpose, Inc.

1. http://www.saturdayeveningpost.com/2010/03/20/archives/then-and-now/imagination-important-knowledge.html.

Chapter 9   Investigation

1. http://www.haagen-dazs.com/company/history.aspx.
2. http://articles.chicagotribune.com/1994-01-28/entertainment/9401280297_1_barnes-noble-superstores-book-discussion-groups-bestseller-list.

Chapter 10   Incubation

1. https://www.cia.gov/news-information/featured-story-archive
/benjamin-franklin.html
2. Keith Sawyer, *Explaining Creativity*, 2nd ed. (New York: Oxford
University Press, 2012). Copyright © 2012 Business Insider, Inc.
All rights reserved. 92513:0912JM
3. http://algonquinroundtable.org/.

Chapter 11   Illumination

1. http://www.scientificamerican.com/article.cfm?id=fact-or-
fiction-archimede.
2. Warren Bennis and Patricia Ward Biederman, *Organizing Genius*
(New York: Basic Books, 1998). Copyright © 1998 Warren
Bennis, Patricia Ward Biederman. Reprinted by permission of
Basic Books, a member of the Perseus Books Group.
3. http://familydoctormag.com/digestive-health/52-bowel-movement-
triggers.html.
4. http://www.leadershipnow.com/creativityquotes.html.
5. http://www.time.com/time/subscriber/article/0,33009,
959634,00.html.

Chapter 12   Illustration

1. Ned Washington and Leigh Harline, "When You Wish Upon
a Star." © 1940 by Bourne Co. (Renewed) All Rights Reserved.
International Copyright Secured ASCAP.
2. Roszak, *The Cult of Information*.
3. http://www.wholefoodsmarket.com/company/declaration.php.

Chapter 13   The Road to Camelot

1. Alan Jay Lerner and Frederick Loewe, "Camelot." © 1960.
Publication and Allied Rights Assigned to Chappell & Co., Inc.
2. http://www.nytimes.com/2006/04/02/opinion/02iht-edrohatyn
.html?_r=1&pagewanted=all.
3. http://www.cfo.com/printable/article.cfm/4007436.

4. http://www.wholefoodsmarket.com/company/declaration.php.
5. Lerner and Loewe, "Camelot."
6. http://www.businessweek.com/bwdaily/dnflash/content/mar2009/db20090316_630496.htm.
7. http://www.time.com/time/business/article/0,8599,1858079,00.html.
8. David Gergen, *Eyewitness to Power: The Essence of Leadership Nixon to Clinton* (New York: Simon & Schuster, 2000). © 2000. Reprinted with permission of Simon & Schuster, Inc.
9. Sisodia, Wolfe, and Sheth, *Firms of Endearment*.
10. http://www.amazon.com/Careers-UniversityRecruiting/b?ie=UTF8&node=203348011.
11. Lerner and Loewe, "Camelot."

Chapter 14   A World on Purpose

1. http://www.rezultsgroup.com/blog/a-memorial-day-tribute.html; http://dcstevens1.wordpress.com/2009/10/21/man-on-the-moon/.
2. http://www.federalreserve.gov/aboutthefed/fract.htm.
3. Speech given at American Society of Newspaper Editors, Washington, DC, January 17, 1925.
4. http://www.historyplace.com/speeches/fdr-first-inaug.htm.
5. http://www.un.org/millennium/declaration/ares552e.htm/.
6. http://www.un.org/millenniumgoals/.
7. http://www.pg.com/en_US/sustainability/reports.shtml.
8. http://www.community.nestle.com/Pages/mdg-landing.aspx.
9. http://www.un.org/en/globalissues/briefingpapers/mdgs/index.shtml.
10. http://www.ushealthiest.org/.
11. Keyes, "Authentic Purpose."
12. Greek origin of *bio* http://www.etymonline.com/index.php?term=bio-&allowed_in_frame=0.
13. Greek origin of *mimesis*, http://www.etymonline.com/index.php?allowed_in_frame=0&search=mimesis&searchmode=none.

Epilogue

1. http://www.usconstitution.net/consttime2.html.
2. Sisodia, Wolfe, and Sheth, *Firms of Endearment*.

Resources

I f you have enjoyed *The Story of Purpose* and would like to create your own, please contact me: jreiman@thinkbrighthouse.com

BrightHouse US website:

www.thinkbrighthouse.com

BrightHouse Brasil website:

www.Brighthousebrasil.com.br

Join our purpose-powered community:

www.dailyjoey.com
www.joeyreiman.com
www.facebook.com/BrightHouseATL
@BrightHouseATL

About the Author

Named one of the 100 people who will change the way the world thinks by *Fast Company*, Joey Reiman is chief executive officer (CEO) and founder of the global consultancy company BrightHouse, a company whose sole purpose is to bring soul to the world of business.

Father of ideation, a term he coined, Reiman has emerged as the subject matter expert in the area of purpose-inspired leadership, marketing, and innovation.

His breakthrough purpose methodology and frameworks have been adopted by the likes of Procter & Gamble, The Coca-Cola Company, McDonald's, and many other Fortune 500 companies across the globe.

Reiman is a professor at the Goizueta School of Business at Emory University, where he teaches tomorrow's executives his revolutionary theories and applications for purpose-inspired profit.

His wildly popular business book, *Thinking for a Living*, spawned an ideas movement, and this book, *The Story of Purpose*, promises to bring business back for good.

Winner of hundreds of awards, including the Cannes Lion and Corporate Marketing Leader of the Year.

A world-renowned speaker, Reiman has inspired hundreds of thousands of leaders to move from seller to server, even healer of society. Through his ability to engage an audience with relatable experiences and motivational messages and to take his speeches that extra step, Reiman makes a speaking opportunity not only a memorable one but a meaningful one as well. He takes you on a journey to expand your imagination and become inspired, empowered, and purposeful.

In April 2012, Reiman was the Graham Executive in Residence at the University of the South, which is a distinct honor that only a handful of individuals have received. These select individuals include the founder and CEO of Southwest Airlines, the president of Lionsgate entertainment studio, and the president and CEO of Gulf Oil. In August 2012, Reiman was the recipient of the first Maynard Jackson Youth Foundation Ladder Award, demonstrating a consistent commitment to learning by helping others climb the educational ladder to achieve success.

Reiman says his greatest accolade is his self-proclaimed title of *famillionaire*, a person whose real wealth is in his or her family. He is married to women's activist Cynthia Good. They created two amazing sons, Alden and Julien.

Acknowledgments

The Story of Purpose has many chapters, the first being my own search for meaning. I found it when I met my wife, Cynthia. She is my reason for being. For 23 years, she has been my "once upon a time."

Our two sons, Alden and Julien, are the result of two people crazy in love. Their souls and smiles show it. Alden is acing his freshman year at Brandeis University and Julien is a junior at Galloway High School in pursuit of his own beautiful story.

My thanks to Robyn Spizman, who is no stranger to success. Both visionary and cheerleader, Robyn has inspired and guided me every step of the way, authoring a library of books herself. Ali Spizman is her dauntless daughter, my executive assistant, and a rock star. Also an author, Ali worked tirelessly on this book while working around the clock at BrightHouse. I know of no associate more skilled, willed, and thrilled with her life and work, and it shows every day. Robyn's other jewel is her son, attorney and writer Justin Spizman, who has contributed to this book as well.

My literary agent is Jackie Meyer. There is no one more genuine, knowledgeable, and direct in the game of publishing. The world would be better read if all authors had her company, Whimsy, representing them.

John Wiley & Sons wrote the book on books. My amazing editor Lauren Murphy is a hero in this story. She saw this work as a way to make the world work better. I was the first benefactor, as I learned so much. Thank you for believing in this book. And Christine Moore, thank you for helping me develop this story. On the back end, thank you to Lydia

225

Dimitriadis, Susan Moran, and Heather Condon for helping bring this book to life. Your encouragement kept me on point and on time. Thank you to the legal departments who worked tirelessly to refine content.

And *thank you* to the bright thinkers at BrightHouse, the world's first ideation company. These purpose pioneers made BrightHouse a global name among the world's best companies and made considerable contributions to *The Story of Purpose*.

Leading the charge was chief creative officer, poet, and painter Cathy Carlisi, who helped me turn the advertising industry upside down two decades ago and is now back to do the same for business. Her artistic sense is that of nature, and her pen a paintbrush, as is evident in many of the creative examples in this book.

Chief strategy officer Dolly Meese redefined what a consultancy can and should do for business. For the past six years, Dolly has brought the frameworks in this book to dozens of businesses around the world. I know of no other strategist who commands the respect she is given by our clients.

Chief financial officer Kim Rich proved that you could make money with meaning. While keeping her watchful eye on the numbers, Kim's other eye was on the content of this book and its completion.

Ashley Lewis produces every day, writes every day, and dances every day. She deserves much applause for many of the examples in this story and a standing ovation for her wit and wherewithal.

Monika Nikore is our senior strategist in Atlanta. Her thoughtfulness is what this story is all about. She came to BrightHouse to change the world. The results are in *The Story of Purpose*.

Maggie Schear is our senior strategist in Cincinnati, Ohio, but her light shines all the way to Atlanta and beyond. I write about Maggie with some trepidation because if I were to describe her mind and spirit, one of you readers would try to steal her from BrightHouse. So I am just going to say she is Madam Curie and Mother Teresa combined.

Special thanks to Justin Baum, our creative director, who directed many of the illustrations, and to Mary Jane Cooper for keeping the house running while I was running around and writing.

Thanks to the rest of BrightHouse, to our summer interns Manya Cherabuddi, Caroline Rogers, and Pedro Henrique, and fall interns Caroline Tanner and Amanda Wikman; I had the honor of their super support right up to deadline.

Obrigado to BrightHouse Brasil. Leaders Jaime and Cecilia Troiano, Fabio Milnitzky, and Marie-Océane Gazurek have built a thriving business in Brasil. Brazilians love purpose and are natural storytellers. Hopefully, this book will be translated into Portuguese for so many of my friends, including those at Bank Itaú, who were kind enough to share their story of purpose with me.

Andrea Hershatter is dean and director of the BBA program at Emory University's Goizueta School of Business. She is responsible for my position as professor there and for much of the body and spirit of this work. Andrea was BrightHouse's first chief learning officer. Her teachings are a lesson for all of business and the world.

To my Emory teaching assistants, thank you for all contributions. To my students in Ideation 441, you are my favorites.

The Story of Purpose could not have made it into your hands without the stories that were put into mine. Thank you Bob McDonald, Bruce and Nancy Brown, and Marc Pritchard.

My gratitude also goes to purposeful Procter & Gamble (P&G) leaders Greg Icenhower and Paul Fox; Harley Procter marketing director Daniel Epstein; Matt Carcieri; Lisa Hillenbrand; Patrick-Lockwood Taylor; Marusia Diaz;

James Illingworth; Ammie Walter; Brad Lenning; Matt Hollenkamp; Michelle Potorski; Michelle Robbins; Courtney Bott; Tara Brown; Taylor Montgomery; Michele Baeten; Mark Murrison; Lynn Cobb; Monica Rojas; Tracey Long; Heather Valento; and P&G archivists Ed Rider and Shane Meeker.

To all of you, I dedicate the following:

The TIDE of Purpose Raises All Brands.

Purpose is the FUSION of intention and contribution. Its SCOPE reaches far and wide, and its BRAUN is great. Until now, purpose was a SECRET you might say that was locked in an IVORY tower. But like a COMET from VENUS, purpose has created a CASCADE of new opportunity as we ALIGN all our brands to bring JOY to people's lives. Purpose LUVS people. It PAMPERS us by brightening our days with CHEER. And it provides a SAFEGUARD for those tough times when we wish things were more NICE N EASY. Purpose PUFFS up our chests, puts BOUNCE in our step and PERT in our smiles. Purpose is putting Procter & Gamble HEAD & SHOULDERS above its competitors, creating a BOUNTY where all stakeholders GAIN. Purpose is the DAWN of an ERA in marketing. And P&G brand builders are riding its CREST. We know people want more meaning in their lives and a good DASH of purpose ALWAYS delivers.

Also a special shout out to my dear friend and world-famous swimmer Diana Nyad, who helped the Secret brand discover purpose and is inspiring millions to find their own.

To my dearest friend and eight-time purpose pioneer Jay Gould and his inseparable, wonderful wife Arlene Gould, and to my colleague Jeannette Long and her associates at American Standard.

To Newell Rubbermaid's Michael Polk, Mark Ketchum, David Doolittle, Bill Burke, Ted Woehrle, Penny McIntyre,

Kristie Juster, Mike Halak, AJ Ross, Neil Eibeler, Curt Rahilly, and Jim Poppins for creating brands that truly matter to the world.

Many thanks to The Coca-Cola Company's Brian Dyson, Sandy Douglas, Katie Bayne, and Stuart Kronauge. Thanks to McDonald's founder Fred Turner; Kevin Newell and Neil Golden; and SunTrust's Bill Rogers, Rilla Delorier, Chuck Allen, and Ken Carrig for your trust in me and BrightHouse's process of purpose.

To the first client who put their trust in BrightHouse, Domino's; Nestlé chief marketing officer (CMO) Tom Buday; former president of Red Lobster Edna Morris; Sapient independent director Jim Bensen; former president of MetLife Lisa Weber; consultant Lauren Masetelli; AIG chief executive officer (CEO) Bob Benmosche; WellPoint CMO Kate Quinn; Cinnabon's CEO Kat Cole; The Home Depot's CEO Frank Blank and CFO Carol Tomé; Carlsberg's Juergen Bull, Anne-Marie Skov, and Khalil Younes; FedEx's Laurie Tucker and Brian Adams; Delta Air Line's Tim Mapes; Southwest Airlines' senior vice president Ginger Hardage; The University of the South's vice chancellor John McCardell; and Chip Manning. To my colleagues at The Boston Consulting Group Mike Deimler and CEO Rich Lesser, Monitor Consulting's former CEO Bob Lourie and uber-consultant Sandi Pocharski, Boston Market "Big Chicken" George Michel, Captain D's CEO Phil Greifeld, Sun Capital's Rodger Krouse and Marc Leder, and Canyon Ranch CEO Mel Zuckerman. To Georgia Pacific CEO Jim Hannen and his colleagues Kathy Walters, Steve Church, and Sheila Widenman. Brandeis University President Fred Lawrence, Dean of Goizueta Business School Larry Benveniste, Professor of Marketing Jag Sheth, Associate Professor of Finance Jeff Rosensweig, and Associate Professor of Organization and Management Richard Makadok, who are all on a path to greater purpose.

Thank you to my counselors Michael Daily, Steve Dorvee, and Steve Sidman; Tom Schrag; Doug Ross; David Skid; Sam Tuck; Dr. Randy Martin; and Dr. Glenn Maron, whose brilliant dental procedure made reaching my manuscript deadline possible.

To my mentor Al Hampel, who to this day inspires me; my dear friends Joe Paprocki and David Paprocki; and my friend and colleague Philip Kotler. Thank you to my purposeful friends Brian Hankin, Richard and Liz Ward, Doug Levy, astrologer Lorelei Robbins, Michael Greenlees, cartoonist Roz Chast, Charles Brewer, Dr. Robert Sternberg, Garth Tissol, Edie Fraser, the late Maynard Jackson, my partner in B.O.T.H. Erik Vonk, my partners at Hiya Media, founder and chief gifting officer Amanda Bessemer, Paul Woolmington, and writer Jan Schroder. To my brother Michael Reiman; Jeff Cervero; and Scott Gaston, who all have opened doors for me.

More than 300 BrightHouse luminaries have brightened our halls, and I would like to acknowledge those whose brilliance impacted *The Story of Purpose:* Emory University professor involved in neuroscience research in the Department of Psychiatry Dr. Rick Gilkey, philosopher Dr. Sam Keen, anthropologists Dr. Bradd Shore and Dr. Mary Catherine Bateson, sociologist Dr. Corey Keyes, Sister Joan Chittister, astronomer and author Bob Berman, and Dean of Arts and Sciences at Duke University Laurie Patton.

Finally, I want to give great thanks to psychologist Dr. Arthur Cohen, whose thinking and inspiration has found its way into my heart and this book, and to the late professor and author Dr. Theodore Roszak, who believed that the best ideas shaped history and our future as well.

And to God, who created the greatest purpose story of all. Thank God for God!

Index